FRANCIS BACON

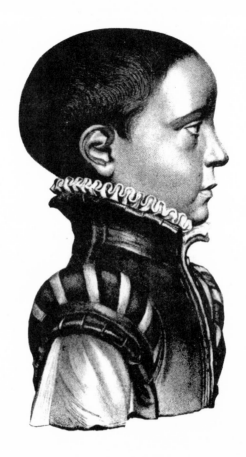

FRANCIS BACON AS A BOY

FRANCIS BACON

A BIOGRAPHY BY
MARY STURT

LONDON
KEGAN PAUL, TRENCH,
TRUBNER & CO. LTD.
BROADWAY HOUSE, CARTER LANE, E.C.

1932

TO

THE PIOUS AND INDUSTRIOUS SHADE

OF

JAMES SPEDDING

THESE PLUMES

PRINTED IN GREAT BRITAIN BY HEADLEY BROTHERS,
109 KINGSWAY, LONDON, W.C.2 ; AND ASHFORD, KENT.

CONTENTS

LIST OF ILLUSTRATIONS

PREFACE

In 1837 Macaulay took up his pen to lay low yet
another of the idols of the past.   He was reviewing a
new edition of Bacon's works, and to the misguided
partiality of the editor Macaulay applied his patron-
izing scorn or brilliant invective.   Secure in the
intellectual triumphs of his age, pure among his
immutable principles, Macaulay can pity and condemn
the noble spirits of all times and nations other than his
own.   " Mr Montagu's faith ", he remarks, " is
sincere and implicit " and his love of his subject
" constantly overflows from his lips and his pen."
Misguided devotion !   Bacon looked at by the clear-
eyed journalist of 1837 was a very different figure.
" His conduct was not always such as an impartial
judge can contemplate with approbation"; and even
worse, "Bacon was a man whose principles were not
strict and whose spirit was not high."   When that has
been said, Bacon is condemned and takes his place
with Cicero, Shakespeare, Fielding and a host more
of overrated beings, who have so cast a spell upon
mankind that they have hidden the basest failings, the
most flagrant lack of principles, under an enchanted
cloud of words.   But words are of no avail before a
Macaulay wedded to disinterested truth.   What is
genius, what the glamour of supreme poetry before a
critic who discerns a lack of principle ?   Bacon and
Shakespeare are banished beyond the same Victorian
pale.

Strangely enough, Macaulay has been believed.
Perhaps because so many passages from the Essays
occur in Greek and Latin prose books, and because so
many labouring and impressionable minds have tried
to convert passages of invective into the echoing
rotundities of Cicero or the more nervous periods
of Demosthenes, few men's ideas of Bacon have a
more solid foundation than the rhetoric of the *Edin-
burgh Review*.   Macaulay surveying the field of Bacon's
character discerns that he had one vice, a vice that
hurled thousands of angels flaming to hell before
ever it toppled Francis from his pedestal.   Bacon was
ambitious, and this most culpable desire to rise in his
profession is the cause of all those blemishes which
Macaulay's eye so easily discerns.

" Had Bacon's civil ends continued to be moderate,
he would have been, not only the Moses, but the
Joshua of philosophy. . . . He would have left, not
only a great, but a spotless name.   Mankind would
then have been able to esteem their illustrious bene-
factor. . . . We should not then have to blush for
the disingenuousness of this most devoted worshipper
of speculative truth, for the servility of the boldest
champion of intellectual freedom.   We should not
then have seen the same man at one time far in the van,
and at another far in the rear of his generation.   We
should not then be forced to own that he who first
treated legislation as a science was among the last
Englishmen who used the rack, that he who first
summoned philosophers to the great work of inter-
preting nature was among the last Englishmen who
sold justice, and we should conclude our survey of a
life placidly, honourably, beneficently passed ' in
industrious observations, grounded conclusions, and

profitable inventions and discoveries ' with feelings
very different from those with which we now turn
away from the checkered spectacle of so much glory
and so much shame." A fine passage, and though
it is the peroration of the Essay it has remained
all that most men know or need to know of Francis
Bacon.

But in fairness to Bacon it must be said that Macaulay was a very bad historian. It is unjust to make a
King's Counsel, without salary and without influence,
responsible for the policy of the government in cases
judged to be of the highest public importance ; and
the history of the Court of Chancery through the next
two centuries gives no indication of that purity which
Macaulay claims for it. Bacon's accusation and
fall had parallels among his own friends and contemporaries. Yelverton was in the Tower only a
month or two before he was, and his enemy Williams
was to spend several years in that gloomy fortress.
Considering the state of parties and political feeling in
1620 Bacon was not particularly unfortunate, and his
fate, if it made men more careful, by no means made
them more honest. Thus Bacon is damned for most
men unheard, at the mouth of a man writing in semi-
ignorance to please the most hypocritical public that
has ever existed.

Bacon, indeed, is not very easy to sum up in the
conventional historian's portrait. The methods of
Tacitus fit him ill. Many men's characters are
consistent or allow of some nicely balanced contradic-
tories. Bacon had a singularly rich personality, but
also one which was singularly consistent with itself.
He was many-sided, but this did not mean a fluctuation
of purpose or confusion. Each strain in him had its

own aims and held to those aims with astonishing persistency through life. If sometimes he mourned that he had not developed one part of himself more fully, that was only the regret which every man of rich potentialities feels for some one of his possible selves. A man of meagre personality can realise himself completely, a man as richly endowed as Bacon can only live one or two lives in the space of sixty-five years; and all the other might-have-beens go un-perfected, a source of regret that one body, one life span, is too brief a space for the full development of so great a spirit.

Lytton Strachey, in his book *Elizabeth and Essex*, has seen something of all this, but he has caught at a phrase from Aubrey and made it into a symbol which, though picturesque, is essentially unjust. Aubrey remarks that Bacon " had a delicate, lively hazel eye. Dr Harvey told me it was like the eye of a viper." Starting from this, Strachey embarks on an estimate of Bacon's character :

" It was not by the juxtaposition of a few opposites, but by the infiltration of a multitude of highly varied elements, that his mental condition was made up. He was no striped frieze ; he was shot silk. The detach-ment of speculation, the intensity of personal pride, and the uneasiness of nervous sensibility, the urgency of ambition, the opulence of superb taste—these qualities blending, twisting, flashing together, gave to his secret spirit the subtle and glittering superficies of a serpent. A serpent, indeed, might well have been his chosen emblem—the wise, sinuous, dangerous creature, offspring of mystery and the beautiful earth. . . . In literature, in spite of the colour and richness of his style, his genius was essentially a prose one.

Intellect, not feeling, was the material out of which his gorgeous and pregnant sentences were made. Intellect ! It was the common factor in all the variations of his spirit ; it was the backbone of the wonderful snake."

Much of this portrait is as true as it is well written, but the word " viper " in Aubrey had left an echo ringing in Mr Strachey's head which betrayed him into a fundamental error. Bacon was not " dangerous ". Probably of all politicians, men of high place and power, he was the kindest, least spiteful and least subtle. He was no intriguer ; he seems always to have put his cards on the table. He attempts, in one of the later books of the *De Augmentis*, to sketch out a science of getting on in the world, but after a maxim or two from the Bible, as that a soft answer turneth away wrath, he has nothing more to say. In the sense in which he intends his new science, he had not got on. He had risen slowly, and he attained his final eminence simply because he was infinitely the ablest Englishman of his day. Had he lived in our age he would have been more successful, more loved and respected. He was out of place in his time and generation, and thus misplaced he was not dangerous. Nor did he wish to be. He was without malice. His only feud was with Coke, and though he contributed somewhat to Coke's fall, his conduct was straightforward and in tune with his general policy. When we contrast the record of his life with that of his cousin Robert Cecil, we can see how pure and honest his actions were.

The really interesting thing about Bacon is that intellectually he was nearly always right. His judgments in all matters, political, scientific or moral, were almost perfect. But those judgments were by no means always acted on. The King rejected his political advice, science lagged behind his vision, and, though he often saw clearly the results of his own conduct, some other element in him drove his feet along the road of which he disapproved. This failure is part of the richness of his character. He was too clever for his age and yet part of it. He could detach himself from the struggle, judge it vain, and then go down into it and contend with the rest. Some men of genius are fortunate in the date of their birth ; others are unlucky. Bacon was among the unfortunates who are born out of due time and can never achieve full harmony with their circumstances.

The century which gave us Macaulay's Essays, the Crystal Palace and the Albert Memorial also gave us the Bacon-Shakespeare controversy. Dr James Wilmot, a country clergyman, seems first to have thought that Shakespeare could not have written the plays that go by his name. The reasons for this conclusion were not very cogent, and the choice of Bacon to father the thus orphaned writings seems to have been prompted rather by admiring affection than by any more logical motive. The same theory germinated independently in America a few years later, and the tree has grown to gigantic proportions. In 1930, Mr Bertram G. Theobald, B.A., published a book of 389 pages proving conclusively that Bacon wrote all the works attributed to Shakespeare, Spenser and Marlowe. He may have written some more, but about these there is no doubt whatever. The demonstration is accomplished by imagining three separate cyphers and

applying them to the letters on the title pages of early
editions. You then get a series of numbers which
add up to the same numbers as could be obtained from
various forms of Bacon's signature, including Fra.
Rosie Cross.

There is one thing which holders of this theory
seem not to have done: they do not appear to have
read the works of any of the authors in dispute.
Above all, they have not read Bacon's works, for in
them is contained a perfect refutation of the whole
theory. Once, when ill, Bacon amused himself by
translating the Psalms. The verse is so execrably
bad that, even allowing for the rather unpromising
subject, it renders it impossible that any of the works
of Shakespeare, Marlowe or Spenser should have
come from his pen. Two verses of the first psalm
are sufficient to prove the point.

> Who never gave to wicked rede
> A yielding and attentive ear;
> Who never sinners' paths did tread,
> Nor sat him down in scorner's chair;
> But maketh it his whole delight
> On law of God to meditate,
> And therein spendeth day and night:
> That man is in a happy state.
>
> He shall be like the fruitful tree,
> Planted along the running spring,
> Which, in due season, constantly
> A goodly yield of fruit doth bring:
> Whose leaves continue always green,
> And are no prey to winter's pow'r:
> So shall that man not once be seen
> Surprised with an evil hour.

A biographer who has loved her subject must
hesitate to bring up such verse against him; but you

cannot argue with a spider's web except by breaking it,
and Bacon cannot be treated as a rational being till
he is freed from these idle romances and superstitious
accretions.

It only remains now to show the real Bacon as
vividly as the records allow.

CHAPTER I

A YOUNGEST SON

IN 1580 a severe frost broke up into a sudden thaw, and citizens of England pushed their windows open to enjoy the delusive warmth. But behind the soft air was chill, and not a few died of this unseasonable exposure. Among others was Nicholas Bacon, Lord Keeper of the Great Seal to Elizabeth, and one of the politicians who directed the early years of her reign.

The manner of his passing illustrates the man. Sir Nicholas, being " under the hands of his barber, and the weather very sultry, had ordered a window before him to be thrown open. As he was become very corpulent, he presently fell asleep in the current of fresh air that was blowing in on him, and awaked after some time, distempered all over. ' Why ', said he to the servant, ' did you leave me thus exposed ? ' The fellow replied that he durst not presume to disturb him. ' Then ', said the Lord Keeper, ' by your civility I lose my life,' and so removed into his bedchamber, where he died a few days after."

He was, as became all good Tudor gentlemen, witty even in the face of death ; and could turn a neat remark on his way to his death-bed, as readily as his predecessor in office, Sir Thomas More, on his way to the scaffold.

For another side to his character, we must look to the Latin summary of his character : " Vir praepinguis, ingenio acerrimo, singulari prudentia, summa eloquentia, tenaci memoria, et sacris conciliis alterum columen."

Burghley was his peer in councils of state, and the husband of his wife's sister; and, had we nothing but Camden's Latin, we should think Nicholas Bacon an inhuman fellow, grossly fat and solemn as a judge.

But he was not. His wit had a double edge that retains its sharpness through the centuries. Over the doorway of his small house at Gorhambury he wrote *Mediocria firma,* and left those that had eyes to see to discern, under a virtuous platitude, a boast directed against the more splendid buildings of his rivals.

If his home was small, the gardens were his pride, and Francis Bacon, his youngest and favourite son, inherited the taste for garden-building.

Nor was he without schemes. In Henry VIII's day educational matters were much discussed, and Nicholas Bacon presented a plan for the foundation of a great college to train statesmen. The students were to learn good Latin and French, public policy, domestic management and foreign negotiation. They were to make historical collections of systems of government, and they were to travel in the suites of the King's ministers. Such a college would have been very different from the universities of England, with their bad Latin and their devotion to a mediævalized Aristotle, and the men that Nicholas desired to train were to be different from the typical products of the universities. Nicholas himself was one of the first modern politicians and civil servants. He was the second layman to hold the office of Lord Keeper (or Lord Chancellor), and his position as a member of the governing council was never strengthened with any

NICHOLAS BACON

title beyond a knighthood. His fellows at the council table were lords and earls, but they came and went; while he and Burleigh, representatives of the new order, where honest intelligence, care and forethought were to be the chief qualifications, remained the props of the nation. The academy that he projected was to train his successors from the upper but not probably the noble classes; and, had the scheme been approved of, and had it been administered in the spirit in which Nicholas saw it, the highly-educated professional civil servant would have come into existence in the sixteenth century instead of the nineteenth.

But, failing the provision of a state school for political studies, he educated his own children along the lines he proposed; and, having educated them, established them in the world with fortunes sufficient to support them as became gentlemen.

The children by his first wife were in no way remarkable; but when he married for the second time Anne Cooke, one of the cleverest and most violent-tempered women in England, the offspring, Anthony and Francis, were both out of the common. Neither was strong, and Francis in particular was noted for a precocious gravity of manner. At thirteen he was sent to Cambridge, and learnt enough of the learning of the day to speak disrespectfully of it ever after; and at sixteen he was sent to France to continue his political studies under the care of Sir Amias Paulet. And there he was, aged nineteen, when his father died, and his mother, taking this event fiercely to heart, as she took all others, summoned him home to consider life.

Francis Bacon was in an unhappy position, and his chief embarrassment was money. His father's scheme of providing for his children had stopped short at himself. For all the others he had bought an estate and given it to them. But though he had accumulated the money for Francis, that untimely thaw and over-punctilious barber had stayed the completion of the plan, and the money not being secured to Francis went with the rest of the estate. This was but law, and Francis did not grumble, though the prospect of earning his own living was even less palatable to him than it is to a child of the upper professional classes today. A gentleman was not then supposed to be hampered in the public service by an absolute need to earn his living, though the rewards that office brought were substantial and highly appreciated. Thus Francis's position was very different from that which even his father had held, and this financial trouble was an incessant anxiety to him for over twenty years.

The natural course for Francis to follow was to become a student at Gray's Inn and so qualify for the legal profession. In going to the Inn he was walking in his father's footsteps. His father had been a member all his life; his brothers had one by one preceded him in the chambers that belonged to the family. The new hall, with its handsome carved screen, open roof of fine beams, stained windows, and all the appurtenances of an Elizabethan hall, had been built largely under his father's direction. As the son of a judge, he had the right to be admitted an ancient of the society at once, without the usual forms and attendance.

Gray's Inn, when Francis entered it, must have been a pleasant place. It was almost in the country, and from the limits of its rough garden and coney garth the view extended up to the low hills of Hampstead and Highgate. It was secluded—the only entrance was from Gray's Inn Lane, a rural thoroughfare, with one or two inns for travellers and their horses—and it was a society dignified, industrious, and concerned with the law of the land—a study which commands respect.

Francis, up to this age, had received an education varied and interesting. He had actually been born at his father's town house in the Strand. Along the river, from Whitehall nearly to St. Paul's, stood a line of great houses whose sites are marked by the names of modern streets:—Northumberland House, York House (the streets representing this are, owing to sad later events, Villiers Street and Buckingham Street), Durham House, Bedford House, Savoy, Somerset House, Arundel House, Essex House, Barnard's Castle. They were cut off from the Strand itself by a row of close-set, timbered houses, and the coaches of their owners dived down narrow turnings or under arches, the horses struggling with the sudden steep slope of the ground, to come out on the wide courtyards of the houses themselves. The houses had all the irregularity of the age. Arundel House was more like a farm than a town mansion. Its courtyard was surrounded by low timbered buildings with outside stairways. Durham House was built on the very edge of the river, its walls rising sheer from the water, its terrace above the stream, with a wall and arched doorways leading to flights of steps; and York House, where Nicholas Bacon lived, stood end on to the river, looking across a regularly patterned flower-garden and a group of trees at the severe walls of Durham House.

It is twenty miles from London to St. Alban's along
Watling Street, and the Bacons' country house stands
in a great park, the slowly-rolling country tree-set,
pleasant and unadventurous. Bacon's taste in land-
scape and music was the same : " I ever loved easy
airs, that go full all the parts together, and not those
strange points of accord and discord," and gardens,
smoothly-flowing water, elm-trees and mild sunshine
were his delight. Gorhambury in spring is lovely,
and to ride down to the lodge gates, with the square-
cut bulk of the cathedral showing on the next hill,
turn off to the right and then to the left along the old
road with the miles of tree-set, easy country between
him and London, was as pleasant an occupation as
any boy could desire.

Both at home and at college he came strongly under
the influence of the reformed religion. His father was
a reasoned and reasonable adherent, his mother an
unreasonable one. The attitude that Francis adopted
through life was that of his father, modified, as the
years passed, by a growing impatience with religious
controversies that occupied men's minds to the
exclusion of more important matters : " I myself am
like the miller of Grancester, that was wont to pray
for peace amongst the willows ; for while the winds
blew, the wind-mills wrought, and the water-mill was
less customed. So I see that controversies of religion
must hinder the advancement of sciences."

His mother's influence, in this as in all else, seems
to have acted mainly by contraries, and no small part
of Francis's character can be derived from this affec-
tionate opposition.

Anne Bacon was for ever in the height of a passion.
It might be a fierce possessive maternal tenderness, an

enthusiastic devotion to a deprived minister, a rough abuse of a servant, or the skilful translating from the Latin of Bishop Jewel's *The Apology for the Church of England*, but it was all done fiercely, and Francis with his grave ways, courteous speech, gentle handling of situations and persons, doubtless, like many another child, made special cultivation of the virtues he missed in his dearest relatives. Such an opposition does not necessarily imply dislike, and Francis never, so far as our record runs, spoke or wrote a harsh word to his mother, and he elected to be buried in the same grave with her in the plain little church at the end of Gorhambury drive. Francis, for all his reason and careful balance of emotions, had touches of the sentimental, and this burial beside his mother, in the church where he had probably listened to his first sermons, and studied the crude painting of the Judgment Day above the chancel arch, is one of them. Another is his devotion to York House, his birthplace, which he seemed to care for with an unreasoning love such as he never gave a human friend.

At Cambridge religion was the live topic of the day. Cartwright, the famous non-conformist, had recently been lecturing, and his lectures caused general scandal. Their content can be imagined from the letter of protest that was sent to Cecil as High Chancellor: " He taught such doctrine as was pernicious and intolerable in a Christian commonwealth: that is, that in the church of England there was no lawful and ordinary calling and choosing or admitting of ministers ; and that the election of ministers and bishops at this day was tyrannous, and that archiepiscopi, decani, archidiaconi, etc., were officia et nomina impietatis."

Cartwright was deprived of his office of Lady Margaret Professor, and soon after of his college fellowship, but from the country he continued to harass the orthodox with his views. In particular he wrote a *Reply* to Dr. Whitgift's *Answer to the Admonition*, and this " Reply, counted so notable a piece of work and wonderfully cried up by the party as unanswerable, consisted in general of two false principles and rotten pillars : whereof the one was, that we must of necessity have the same kind of government that was in the Apostles' time and as expressed in the Scriptures, and no other ; the other was, that we may not in any wise, or on any consideration, retain in the Church anything that hath been abused under the Pope."

To all of which Whitgift " Replied " again. And this was the intellectual excitement when Francis Bacon came up to college.

These stirring ideas stood out in an intellectual world that was otherwise sterile. Mediæval and Renaissance learning had come to a dead stop, and for a period the universities had nothing to offer. Bacon at Cambridge, Hobbes, the friend of his old age, at Oxford, Locke a little later all say the same thing. There was as yet no rift in the clouds of classical night, no star that shone on these young men of the new science that was so soon to be born.

" Discoursing skornfully of the philosophy of the Græcians with some better respect to the Aegiptians, Persians, Caldes, and the utmost antiquity and the mysteries of the poets," wrote Bacon in his private notes about his next book many years later, and Hobbes, penning his words for publication, is as forcible. " But this privilege of Reason is allayed by another, and that is, by the privilege of absurdity, to which no living creature is subject, but men only. And of men, those are of all most subject to it that profess Philosophy." " There is yet another fault in the Discourses of men, which may be numbered among the sorts of madness : that is when men speak such words as, put together, have in them no signification at all, but are fallen upon by some, through misunderstanding of the words they have received, and repeated by rote by others, from the intention to deceive by obscurity. And this is incident to none but those that converse in questions of matters incomprehensible, as the school-men, or in questions of abstruse Philosophy. The common sort of men seldom speak insignificantly, and are therefore by those other egregious persons counted idiots."

For all that, the universities had a difficult task. They were expected to teach Logic, Rhetoric, Philosophy, Metaphysics and Theology to their students ; but the students came up at thirteen or fourteen and left at a correspondingly young age. It was as if the III, IV and V forms of a secondary school had to study Logic and Metaphysics. The only way to do it was to reduce the subjects to the level of the students. Since even if boys of those times developed earlier, we cannot imagine them to have been equal to a full treatment of the subjects. What Logic becomes when reduced to the standard of eighteen years old every Pass man knows. Reduce it two or three years more, so that it can be studied at fifteen, and the barrenness of the subject can be imagined. A subject so arid can only carry disgust to the learner's mind. It was not only the clever student who

turned away intellectually unsatisfied, the stupid man
was nauseated.

Francis left the university convinced that all the
learning of his day was sterile and worthless, and a
vain pursuit of the wrong aims. " Are we the richer
by one poor invention, by reason of all the learning
that hath been these many hundred years ? The
industry of artificers maketh some small improvement
in things invented, and chance sometimes in experimenting maketh us to stumble upon somewhat which
is new; but all the disputation of the learned never
brought to light one effect of nature before unknown.
All the philosophy of nature which is now received is
either the philosophy of the Grecians or that other of
the Alchemists. That of the Grecians hath the
foundations in words, in ostentation, in confutation,
in sects, in schools, in disputations. That of the
Alchemists hath the foundation in imposture, in
auricular traditions and obscurity."

At one time and another Francis was taken by his
father to court, and grew up with the profound
reverence for the Queen which was typical of the age.

To this devotion, learnt direct from his family and
public sentiment, the journey to France added direct
intellectual conviction. France was suffering all the
curses of a weak monarchy, internal disturbances and
financial confusion. A mere résumé of the events
that passed during Francis's stay there are enough to
show what he saw.

In 1576 the Huguenots were in arms and sufficiently
strong to secure an edict giving them toleration and
an arrangement of parliamentary representation. But
the Guises refused to be any party to the arrangement,
and war broke out as usual the next spring. This

time the Protestants were less successful, and the edict which closed this campaigning season was rather more intolerant, but formed a possible *modus vivendi*. However, by 1580 they were once more fighting, capturing a town here and a town there, and ending as usual with an inconclusive peace.

This wretched business, cruel and senselessly recurrent, must have filled all thinking persons with disgust, but the incident which remained most clearly in Francis Bacon's mind occurred in 1588 when he was once more back in England. Paris was practically in revolt against the King, and when he summoned four hundred Swiss guards to the suburbs the citizens sent in alarm for the Duke of Guise, and proceeded to barricade the streets. The Duke arrived, was interviewed by the King, and left the palace. He then gave a demonstration of his power that must have been as mortifying to his King as it was complete. Unarmed he rode through the city, and by his mere presence and word calmed the population and stayed the street-fighting. The King, reduced to a nonentity, took horse and rode away to Chartres. If a subject could behave with all the force of monarch, all hopes of a stable government were at an end.

Francis watched and noted, and when he was back in England wrote a little pamphlet on the *State of Christendom*, which he circulated, hoping that the Queen, or his uncle Burghley, or Mr. Secretary Walsingham would think well enough of it to give him a job. In this he sums up the state of France.

" The division in this country for matters of religion and state, through miscontent of the nobility to see strangers advanced to the greatest charges of the realm, the offices of justice sold, the treasury wasted, the people polled, the country destroyed, hath bred great trouble and like to see more."

The ideas that Francis brought back firmly fixed in his mind—and they remained there because of the extraordinary persistence of that mind—were the importance of a firm monarchy, the heinousness of rebellion, and the necessity of a careful government.

CHAPTER II

THE INNS OF COURT

GRAY'S INN, when Francis joined it, formed part of what was perhaps the best legal university in Europe. The four Inns of Court were societies of students and practising lawyers, with their own buildings, libraries and regulations. Apart from the fact that they were not incorporated, and so could not hold lands and receive money, they resembled the modern Oxford or Cambridge college more closely than anything else of the period. For this reason in particular; the students were older, and the Inns of Court dealt for a large part with young men and not with mere boys.

Their praise was sung by Fortescue, with perhaps a little exaggeration.

" There is both in the Inns of Court and the Inns of Chancery a sort of academy or gymnasium fit for persons of their station, where they learn all kinds of music, dancing and other such accomplishments and diversions, which are called revels, as are suitable for their quality, and such as are usually practised at Court. At other times, out of term, the greater part apply themselves to the study of the law. Upon festival days, and after the offices of the church are over, they employ themselves in the study of sacred and profane history; there everything which is good and virtuous is to be learned, and all vice is discouraged

and banished. So that knights, barons, and the
greatest nobility of the kingdom often place their
children in the Inns of Court, not so much to make
the laws their study, much less to live by the profession,
having large patrimonies of their own, but to form
their manners and to preserve them from the con-
tagion of vice. The only way they have of punishing
delinquents is by expelling them the society, which
punishment they dread more than criminals do
imprisonment and irons."

The students were not always quite as blameless as
he represents them. Every now and then there was a
rag and letters of apology had to be written to the
Sovereign afterwards. There were many rules of life
which were enforced with a fine.

Regulation in dress, 1557. "The companions, save
knights and Benchers, are forbidden to wear on their
doublets and hose any light colours, except scarlets
and crimsons, nor wear any upper velvet cap, or any
scarf or wings on their gown, white jerkyns, buskins
or velvet shoes, double cuffs on their shirts, feathers or
ribbons on their caps, upon pain to forfeit, for the
first default, 3s. 4d. and the second expulsion without
redemption . . ." No one, under the degree of
knight, being in commons, to wear any beard above
three weeks' growing upon pain of 40s. No hat to
be worn in hall at dinner or supper time—fine 3s. 4d.
No boots or spurs to be worn in hall, but they shall
come with their caps " decently and orderly ". No
fellow of the society stand with his back to the fire.

What was the fine for the last offence is not stated,
but there were severe prohibitions against laun-
dresses or other women-servants under the age of
forty years going to the men's rooms.

Meals were in hall, and the usual menu was :— breakfast of bread and beer, dinner of beef or mutton and on Easter Day of eggs and green sauce, supper of bread and cheese with cups of beer.

From this diet Francis Bacon's delicacy revolted, and his admission to the Inn contained the provision that, owing to his health, he might provide himself with a special diet.

The Inns of Court were considered sufficiently important to be the subject of a report by a royal commission, on which Nicholas Bacon sat, and from their report the following description of the Moots, the chief instruments of education, is taken.

" The Reader, with two Benchers, cometh into the hall, and there most commonly one of the utter barristers propoundeth to them some doubtful case, the which every one of the Benchers in their ancienties argue, and last of all he that moved : this done, the Readers and Benchers sit down on the bench in the end of the hall, whereof they take their name, and on a form towards the midst of the hall sitteth down two Inner Barristers and on the other side of them on the same form two Utter Barristers, and the Inner Barristers doe in French openly declare unto the Benchers some kind of Action, the one being as it were retained with the plaintiff in the Action, and the other with the defendent, after which things done, the Utter Barristers argue such questions as be disputable in the case and this ended the Benchers do likewise declare their opinions, how they think the law to be in the same questions. This manner of exercise of moting is daily used during the vacation."

This legal sharp practice, for the question to be discussed was not announced beforehand, had the qualities both of a debate, a tutorial class and a lecture, and was probably highly effective for the purpose of training barristers. In addition during term the members of the Inn would attend the courts and also practise the ordinary work of a solicitor. Bacon can very soon draw a power of Attorney for his brother Anthony, who is abroad, arrange conveyances and discuss all the various forms and formalities of raising money.

But when he first established himself at the Inn he was like other young men of quality, and did not believe that he would have to practise law seriously as a profession. He was the son of a Lord Keeper, the nephew of the Lord Treasurer, a young man of ability, and he felt every confidence that something would turn up. To help it to turn, he addressed himself politely to his uncle and aunt.

To Lady Burghley

My singular Good Lady,

I was as ready to show myself mindful of my duty by waiting on your Ladyship at your being in town as now by writing, had I not feared lest your Ladyship's short stay and quick return might well spare one that came of no earnest errand. I am not yet greatly perfect in ceremonies of court, whereof I know your Ladyship knoweth both the right use and true value. My thankful and serviceable mind shall be always like itself, howsoever it vary from the common disguising. Your Ladyship is wise and of good nature to discern from what mind every action proceedeth, and to esteem it accordingly. This is all the message which my letter hath at this time to deliver, unless it please your Ladyship further to give me leave to make this request unto you, that it would please your Ladyship in your letters wherewith you visit my good Lord to vouchsafe the mention and recommendation of my suit, wherein your Ladyship shall bind me more unto you than I can look ever to be able sufficiently to acknowledge. Then in humble manner I take my leave of your Ladyship, committing you as daily in my prayers

LORD BURGHLEY

so likewise in this present to the merciful providence of the Almighty.

> From G. Inn, this 16 Sep., 1580.
> Your Ladyship's most dutiful and bounden nephew,
>
> B. Fra.

To Lord Burghley

My singular Good Lord,

My humble duty remembered and my humble thanks presented for your Lordship's favour and countenance, which it pleased your Lordship at my being with you to vouchsafe me above my degree and desert, my letter hath no further errand but to commend unto your Lordship the remembrance of my suit which then I moved unto you, whereof it also pleased your Lordship to give good hearing so far forth as to promise to tender it unto her Majesty, and withal to add in the behalf of it that which I may better deliver by letter than by speech, which is, that although it must be confessed that the request is rare and unaccustomed, yet if it be observed how few there be which fall in with the study of common laws, either being well left or friended, or at their own pre-election, or forsaking likely success in other studies of more delight and no less preferment, or setting hand therunto early without waste of years ; upon such survey made, it may be that my case may not seem ordinary, no more than my suit, and so more beseeming unto it. As I force myself to say this in excuse of my motion, lest it should appear unto your Lordship altogether indiscreet and unadvised, so my hope to obtain it resteth only upon your Lordship's good affection towards me and grace with her Majesty, who methinks needeth never to call for the experience of the thing, where she hath so great and so good a person which recommendeth it. According to which trust of mine, if it may please your Lordship both herein and elsewhere to be my patron, and to make account of me as one in whose well-doing your Lordship hath interest, albeit indeed your Lordship hath had place to benefit many, and wisdom to make due choice of lighting-places for your goodness, yet do I not fear any of your Lordship's former experiences for staying my thankfulness born in heart, howsoever God's good pleasure shall enable me or disable me outwardly to make proof thereof. For I cannot account your Lordship's service distinct from that which I owe to God and my Prince, the performance whereof to best proof and purpose is the meeting-point and rendez-vous of all my thoughts. Thus I

2

take my leave of your Lordship in humble manner, committing you, as daily in my prayers, so likewise in this present to the merciful protection of the Almighty.

From G. Inn, this 16 of September, 1580.

Your most dutiful and bounden nephew,

B. FRA.

Two very pretty and proper letters, Francis must have thought, when he had copied them fair and sent them off, and much time and thought their composition must have cost him, for they were his first efforts in the line, and it was only as the years went by that he acquired his full skill in letters of this kind.

Bacon was less well-placed than the young man in his position today. No posts were then advertised, while the disposal of offices went by favour and the words of the great at court. Thus it happened that many a disappointed suitor broke his heart waiting for the office that was ever promised and ever delayed. It is an impersonal matter to write out one's merits for a selection committee; it is another thing to urge one's claims again and again to a man one knows well. Bacon wrote to his uncle in the style of the day, but he also wrote honestly and with a certain dignity, and that honesty is shown by the constancy with which the same sentiments are repeated in varying circumstances for years. " I cannot account your Lordship's service distinct from that which I owe to God and my Prince." Later the same thought is in his mind when he makes his famous reservation to Essex, when he fears the duties will fall separately; but never in all his dealings with patrons or friends does he forget the order in which his duties stood.

Unfortunately these pretty letters were doomed to failure, and the reason is a personal one that was

beyond Bacon's control.   Burghley too had a son—
Robert Cecil, like Francis the youngest of the family,
like him in age, delicacy and intelligence, and like him
further in that his elder half-brother was a man of no
intellectual ability.   Thomas Cecil, soldier and country gentleman, who seems to have been fitted for the
life of a hard-riding squire rather than an earldom, was
clearly no successor to his father, and on the younger
lame Robert the family hopes were fastened.   Perhaps his father knew that he was less brilliant than
his cousin, his health was worse and he was lame.
In any case, there was to be no rivalry, and Burghley
spoke Francis fair, and saw to it that no promotion
should come his way till he had placed his own son
in a position so high and secure that he could not be
dislodged or overtopped.

At first Francis bore the delay well.   He was above
all things busy.   He was working hard at law and
rising in estimation at the Inn.   He had become a
Member of Parliament for Melcombe in Dorsetshire,
and he had begun to write on public matters.

His first paper is called *Notes on the State of Christendom* and enumerates the different states of Europe,
giving brief information about each concerning such
matters as the rulers, finance and general condition
of the country.   It is brief, covering all Europe in
thirteen pages, but it represents an amount of knowledge that could not have been acquired without
considerable labour.   The importance of the paper
from Bacon's point of view was that it should have
marked him out as a useful man.   Part of the duties of
the Secretary of State was the collection of information
about other countries, and this information was
supplied by correspondents, digested at home by

competent assistant secretaries, and supplied to him
ready for use at the council table. Anthony Bacon
was abroad, acting somewhat in the first capacity.
How nice, thought Francis, if he could obtain a post
under Walsingham in the second. This paper was
to show how neatly he could summarize and present.
Unfortunately the paper failed of its effect.

Then he tried his pen on the Queen, and in a
carefully reasoned exposition set out his views on the
proper treatment of the Roman Catholics. It is a
paper of extreme good sense and moderation and in
short amounts to this, that they should be treated
with mildness, in order that they may not be driven
to the courage of despair, while at the same time their
numbers may be decreased by better provision for
the education of children and young people in the
doctrines of the Church of England.

It was a remarkable document at a time when the
Queen's life was daily in danger from Roman Catholic
assassins, and while the Armada grew like a thunder-
cloud in the harbours of Spain.

He followed it by an equally reasonable and
moderate discussion of the furious quarrel raging
between the established Church and the more extreme
reformers, saying in effect that both sides had been
in the wrong, and that if they would behave with
courtesy, moderation and tolerance all might yet be
well.

The impression of all these papers is that they came
from the pen of an old, cautious man, and one has
even been ascribed to Burghley as fitting more aptly
with his white beard. Though Bacon was well under
thirty, he never seems, so far as literature is concerned,
to have had any youth. He never expressed a violent

opinion ; he never wrote verse—at least, not till he was on his deathbed—; and when he writes to advise a young friend about his reading he has much to say about historians, but "for poets I can commend none, being resolved to be ever a stranger to them ". His most characteristic work—his essays, begun in his youth, completed in his age, shows everywhere the same concise experience, so different from the florid fantasies of Sidney or Euphues. He was not even, so far as our knowledge goes, in love. No fair face disturbed the solemn cadences of his sentences on church government. He even shut himself up and denied himself to his friends while he searched for information or a cogent argument.

Mr. Faucet, his brother's friend, calling to ask if he should forward any letters, was received coldly.

"I was yesterday at Gray's Inn upon occasion, when I would not fail to call in. But I was answered, by his servant, that he was not at leisure to speak with me, and therefore you must excuse me if I cannot tell you how your mother and friends do at this present. . . . This strangeness which hath at other times been used towards me by your brother hath made me sometimes to doubt that he greatly mistaketh me."

The realm in which his youth did show was a purely intellectual one. He was nursing schemes that for magnificence have seldom been equalled. They obsessed him. He read widely by day to acquire knowledge, and thought it all over at night, with the result that he got up late in the morning. His mother had no patience with such goings-on, and expressed herself with great definiteness to Anthony.

"I verily think your brother's weak stomach to digest hath been much caused and confirmed by untimely going to bed, and then musing *nescio quid* when he should sleep, and then in consequent by late rising and long lying in bed; whereby his men are made sloathful and himself continueth sickly."

These "nescio quids" of maternal disapproval were nothing less than the reform of all human knowledge.

"I confess", writes Francis, "that I have as vast contemplative ends as I have moderate civil ends: for I have taken all knowledge to be my province; and if I could purge it of two sorts of robers, whereof the one with frivolous disputations, confutations and verbosities, the other with blind experiments and auricular traditions and impostures hath committed so many spoils, I hope I should bring in industrious observations, grounded conclusions, and profitable inventions and discoveries, the best state of that province."

Thus shutting himself up by day, lying late abed, going on his daily walks absorbed in the dream of a new science, he was naturally unpopular, and Burghley, importuned afresh, administered a smart avuncular snub. Bacon's answer is the plea of every proud young man with unusual interests and conscious of powers that society will not as yet allow him to use.

My very good Lord,

I take it as an undoubted sign of your Lordship's favour unto me that being hardly informed of me you took occasion rather of good advice than evil opinion thereby. . . .

Indeed I find in my simple observation that they which live as it were *in umbra* and not in public or frequent action, how moderately and modestly soever they behave themselves, yet *laborant invidia*. I find also that such persons as are of nature bashful (as myself is) whereby they want that plausible familiarity which others have, are often mistaken for proud. But this I know well and I must humbly beseech your Lordship to believe, that arrogancy and overweening is so far from my nature, as if I think well of myself in anything it is in this that I am free from the vice. And so wishing unto your Lordship all honour and to myself continuance of your good opinion with mind and means to deserve it, I humbly take my leave.

Gray's Inn, this 6th day of May, 1586.

Your Lordship's most bounden nephew,

FR. BACON.

Chapter III

THE ALLIANCE WITH ESSEX

Perhaps because of his uncle's remonstrance, perhaps because of external circumstances, Francis Bacon's life gradually became wider and more public. For one thing he was growing older. " I wax now somewhat ancient," he wrote in expostulation to his uncle; " one and thirty years is a good deal of sand in the hour-glass," and in that age of early promotion it seemed even more than it does now. Sidney " lived and loved " and fought and fell all before he was thirty-two, and left an imperishable name. Shakespeare had become the world's greatest playwright in twenty-six years. Bacon at thirty-one was a young man without fame or fortune, and with nothing in prospect, but the reversion of a sinecure office that like " another man's ground buttailing upon his house, might mend his prospect but did not fill his barn." Still years, if they did not bring success, brought better health and increased self-confidence.

Moreover, the Queen had discovered that he was useful. He could write. Among his contemporaries he had a prose style which was lucid, unaffected and elegant. He could marshal an obscure argument so that it appeared of the most transparent simplicity, and he could write a defence of a complicated and not too honest policy so that he seemed to be describing the necessary action of eternal laws. From the moment somewhere in 1589, when Elizabeth discovered this power existing in the grave and not too attractive young Bacon, till the time of her death, his pen was always in request to defend or explain the government's actions. Sometimes these statements were for export, and one of the earliest was written over Walsingham's signature and sent to France to influence opinion there in the matter of the treatment of the English Catholics. Others were for use at home, and after the execution of Essex it was to Bacon that the duty fell of drawing up a full account of the " Practices and Treasons Attempted and Committed by Robert, Late Earl of Essex." The Queen herself revised the work in great detail, but Bacon's head planned and his pen found words. As he was still without formal position, not a leader in any sphere, this very important task can only have been given to him because he was outstandingly the most suitable man to perform it.

If he was to be government apologist, he must necessarily come into closer touch with the court, and this he did. He attended court and became ever increasingly intimate with the Queen. She would walk and talk with him, receive and consider his opinion on points of policy, and make jokes, somewhat coarse, after her manner.

But he never received an appointment that carried financial gain. He became one of the Queen's Council and therefore was employed on Crown legal business, but that office, though involving work, was unpaid, so that Bacon's attendance at court, his expenditure on clothes, carriages, and the wear and tear to his household gear in moving now here, now there round London, involved him in ever-increasing

debt. He did what he could to economize and wrote
to his mother :

"It may be I shall have occasion . . . to visit
the court this vacation . . . in which respect,
because cartage of stuff to and fro spoileth it, I would
be glad of that light bed of striped stuff which your
ladyship hath, if you have not otherwise disposed
of it."

But it was not of much avail, especially as it was
part of the duties of a courtier to give the Queen
expensive presents of jewels or embroidered garments
on New Year's Day or her birthday.

Besides this court life, he now had his brother
Anthony back from his travels. Anthony had been
abroad for ten years, studying foreign countries, and
he returned in bad health, crippled with gout, but
possessed of great knowledge and having established
a system of able intelligencers who would keep him
informed of all interesting developments. His absence
abroad had tried his mother almost past bearing.
When money had to be raised for him, Francis
conducted the business without reference to their
mother, who " through passion and grief could scant
endure to intermeddle in any of his business ". The
lady's chief fear was that her son should become
tainted with the Catholicism of the countries of his
sojourning, and above all she suspected his servant
Lawson, whose religion was in doubt. When Lawson
was sent over to England with some confidential
letters, Lady Bacon had him arrested and intercessions
on his behalf failed. This is the account of how
Anthony's emissary in the matter fared.

" Upon my arrival at Gorhambury my Lady used
me courteously until such time I began to move her

for Mr. Lawson, and, to say the truth, for yourself; being so much transported with your abode there that she let not to say that you are a traitor to God and your country; you have undone her; you seek her death; and when you have that you seek for, you shall have but a hundred pounds more than you have now.

"She is resolved to procure her Majesty's letter to force you to return, and when that should be, if her Majesty gave you your right or desert, she should clap you up in prison. She cannot abide to hear of you, as she saith, nor of the other especially, and told me plainly that she should be the worse this month for my coming without you, and axed me why you could not have come from thence as well as myself.

"I am sorry to write it; it is vain to look for Mr. Lawson's return, for these are her Ladyship's own words. 'No, no,' saith she. 'I have learned not to employ ill to good, and if there were no more men in England, and although you should never come home, he shall never come to you.'

"My Lady said she had rather you made the wars with the King of Navarre than to have stayed so long idle in Martoban, and with great earnestness, also tears in her eyes, she wished that when she heard of Mr. Selum's imprisonment you had been fairly buried, provided you had died in the Lord. In my simple judgment she spoke it in her passion, and repented immediately afterwards.

"Thus much I must confess unto you for a conclusion, that I have never seen nor never shall see a wise Lady, an honourable woman, a mother, more perplexed for her son's absence than I have seen that honourable dame for yours."

Such bursts of maternal impatience died down somewhat when she actually had her way and Anthony returned to England. She sent a messenger to meet him, carrying a letter of welcome. But it was a strange letter full of advice of the Polonius kind— "Be not speedy of speech nor talk suddenly, but where discretion requireth, and that soberly, then." Complaining of his past negligence—"Remember you have no father, and you have little enough, if not too little regarded your kind and no simple mother's wholesome advice from time to time"—and ending with an exhortation connected with her chief pre-occupation. "I trust you with your servants use prayer twice in the day, having been where reformation is (i.e. Anthony had been in Geneva). Omit it not for any. It will be your best credit to serve the Lord duly and reverently, and you will be observed at the first now. Your brother is negligent herein, but do you well and zealously, it will be looked for of the best learned sort, and that is the best."

Francis meanwhile was preparing his brother's chambers in the same block as his own. The chief merit of the rooms seems to have been that they were "low and warm", and later the brothers obtained leave to build on additional rooms over their present chambers and the library, provided that the latter was left "of a convenient and proportionate height".

Anne Bacon, with her sons both close at hand, riding out to visit her with fair frequency, and above all making certain demands on her care, was a much happier woman. She lost her temper with others, but not with them. Instead she busied herself in picking and sending them the best strawberries, even arranging them so that the ripest were on top ready to be eaten first, or despatched pigeons for their dinner as the seasons served. But her able, managing mind, beating itself out on matters that were too small for it, could not rest even here, but must go planning every detail. She tells her sons how large a tip they should give to the servants who carried the provisions— sixpence to the boy who came on horseback and was to be sent back the same day ; a shilling to Peter the cook, who " had a good will to carry them on foot ". She advises when their men-servants should drink wine and when not, and she wants to know all the why and wherefore of the use made of the family coach when they went to court. She would have been, like many another woman, wasted for lack of scope had she had more self-control. She had none, and this defect led to the insanity which is imagined to have occupied the last years of her life. Nothing could indicate her state more clearly than the complaint of a servant written to Anthony, partly to explain his conduct, partly in the hope of sympathy :—

" My humble duty remembered unto your good Worship, I thought good to write unto you to satisfy you how unquiet my Lady is with all her household. Edward Yates sent a graenen bitch to Redbourn, and Mr. Lawson sent her to me to keep. And as soon as my Lady did see her, she sent me word she should be hanged. Now I had thought to send her to Kepein. Now by-and-by she sent word by Cros that if I did not take her away she should not sleep in her bed, so indeed I hung her up, whereat she was very angry, and said I was framsey, and bade me go home to my master and make him a fool, I should make none of her."

There were other episodes no less violent, one about a hawk, when the poor correspondent had to go to bed without his supper, and his final complaint is touching in its suggestion of his discomfort.

" I have not given no more cause than I have now told your Worship. And to yield my duty, what I am able I will, but not willing to be here unless she would be quiet. She make me to buy starch and soap to wash my linen withal, more than was wont to be, yet I care not so she would be quiet.

Your servant to command for ever,

EDWARD SPENCER."

The chief cause of the change in Francis Bacon's way of life was his friendship with Essex. Walter Devereux, father of the more famous Robert, had failed in Ireland, that grave of Elizabethan reputations, and perished, not perhaps without the satisfaction of Leicester, who married his widow. Robert, after being sent to Trinity College, Cambridge, Bacon's old college, had come to court under his stepfather's ægis, and succeeded to his position. He was a very handsome youth, with a wide forehead and delicately-shaped head, and he was conspicuous for his learning and literary taste, his courage, and a charming youthful impetuosity. Francis Bacon was rapidly attracted by the man, some seven years younger than he, and knew how to inspire an attachment in return. Bacon seems undoubtedly to have liked young men, especially if they were handsome and likely to rise, and he could establish pleasant relationships with them. Notice from an older man of such distinction must have been flattering, and Bacon knew how to be useful. To whatever topic he gave his mind, he gave it fully, and it was one of the most efficient minds of the age.

This mind he now put at Essex's service. " I did many years since ", wrote Bacon later, " dedicate my travels and studies to the use and (as I may term it) service of my Lord of Essex, which, I protest before God, I did not, making election of him as the likeliest means of mine own advancement, but out of the humour of a man that ever, from the time I had any use of reason, I loved my country more than was answerable to my fortune, and I held at that time my Lord to be the fittest instrument to do good to the state, and therefore I applied myself to him in a manner that I think happeneth rarely among men, for I did not only labour carefully and industriously in that he set me about, whether it were matter of advice or otherwise, but neglecting the Queen's service, mine own fortune, and in a sort my vocation, I did nothing but devise and ruminate with myself to the best of my understanding, propositions and memorials of anything that might concern his Lordship's honour, fortune or service. And when not long after I entered into this course, my brother, Master Anthony Bacon, came from beyond the seas, being a gentleman whose ability the world taketh knowledge of for matters of state, especially foreign, I did likewise knit his service to be at my Lord's disposing." And in return for these services he received from Essex " love, trust and favour ", and finally a gift of land which Bacon " sold for £1,800 to Master Reynold Nicholas ", and thought was worth more, the gift being made " at such a time, and with so kind and noble circumstances, as the manner was as much as the matter ".

This is his account of the relationship written looking back on it nearly ten years later, when events

had run their course.   To Bacon at the time things
must have seemed rather different.   Bacon in 1590
was seeking earnestly for the means of promotion.
Burghley had failed him ; and, though he continued
to hold out hopes, Francis can have had no particular
expectation of efficient help from him.   This was an
age of patrons, and Francis was doing the obvious
thing in attaching his fortune to that of the brilliant
court favourite.   It is much to the credit of all parties
that Bacon could look back on the relationship with so
much satisfaction and so clear a sense that if he gave
he received affection and consideration in return.
There is a very different note in Shakespeare's remonstrance to *his* patron, the vain, volatile and brawling
Earl of Southampton :

> Being your slave, what should I do but tend
> Upon the hours and times of your desire ?
> I have no precious time at all to spend,
> Nor services to do, till you require.
> Nor dare I chide the world-without-end hour
> Whilst I, my sovereign, watch the clock for you,
> Nor think the bitterness of absence sour
> When you have bid your servant once adieu :
> Nor dare I question in my jealous thought
> Where you may be, or your affairs suppose,
> But like a sad slave, stay and think of nought
> Save, where you are, how happy you make those.
> So true a fool is love that in your will,
> Though you do anything, he thinks no ill.

Southampton and Essex were both young favourites
of the court, friends and deeply linked in the same
enterprises, but whereas Southampton kept the poets
and dramatists in his train, and received the dedications
of Venus and Adonis and the Rape of Lucrece, Essex
and Bacon discussed theories of government and the
nature of the " military art ".

The first and greatest service Bacon rendered Essex was to give him a serious place in politics. Essex had already seen some military service in Holland and distinguished himself. He had been Master of the Horse in 1587 and General in 1588. In 1589 he had gone off on an unauthorized expedition to Portugal, but had been received with favour on his return. He now looked to a place at the council table and sought opportunities of yet greater distinction.

Of all business, foreign affairs were the most pressing, and it was in these that the Bacons could best help him. In consequence, it was no long time before the benefit of Anthony's foreign experience was transferred from the Cecils to Essex and the two brothers formed the heads of a kind of miniature foreign office that worked in Essex's house. They retained their rooms in Gray's Inn and day by day must have gone up and down Chancery Lane between the Inn and the Strand, and blessed the stone paving laid not so long ago at the cost of Lincoln's Inn.

This Elizabethan intelligencing combined various modern departments into one. The men employed were secret service agents, spies, almost consuls on occasion. They received pensions from England, they went disguised or under assumed names, or when more convenient openly presented themselves to mayors of towns, obtained an entré to court, or procured passports for each other. The most curious fact, and one which speaks highly for the devoted patriotism of the Elizabethan Englishman, was that some of them were exiles from their own country because of their religion, and actually served the ministers and government that persecuted them. Thus on many occasions their reports of foreign events are interspersed with pleas for tolerance at home.

One of these agents was Anthony Standen, who had left England for the sake of his religion, but had not lost his loyalty. He writes to Burghley: "The year '88, which was the time that huge Armada went and perished, I was by order at the court of Lisbon, where I had a view of all and by the way of Italy, gave advice of the whole matter of their designs, which by the letters I found in Florence seemed to be grateful to her Majesty. Thence proceeded the persuasion he used with me to procure this last time my return again into Spain, which accordingly I did put into execution. . . . Which considered, I do humbly intreat your honour to move her Majesty, as well touching my relief as about my relaxation, and that in such wary sort as it may not appear to Spain by any favour from you, whither, if it be her Highness's liking, I intend to return, and continue, as heretofore, in faithful service and devotion to her Majesty, and to her realm, as the land wherein I was born, and which above all other soils I love."

These men came and went through Italy and Spain, France and the Netherlands. They haunted the courts, drifted up and down the coasts noting the preparations in Spanish harbours, and the sea skirmishes on the coasts of Brittany. They lay with the armies before Chartres and were charged to express the views of the English government to the French council.

"And therefore you shall use all the means you have, both towards Marshal Biron and any other of the King's council, to induce him to continue and speedily attempt that matter."

Anthony Bacon in his years abroad had got to know many of them and had helped some. He returned to England able to place at Essex's disposal either the entire service of these men or else, if they still continued to correspond direct with Burghley, he persuaded them to send duplicates of their dispatches to Essex. It must have been no small mortification to the Cecil faction to find that a court rival shared information that they had regarded as exclusive.

This system of intelligence was not confined to statesmen. Anyone who was rich enough and had sufficiently wide interests provided himself with information in the same way. The most famous example of the day was the great financial house of Fugger at Augsburg. There to the Golden Counting House came letters from all over the world, even from Goa, then a six months' journey away, and many of these letters were preserved in a cabinet whose compartments are labelled with the names of towns and decorated with views of the cities from which the letters came.

Less princely traders had less perfect sources of information, and many a man who lived away from the capital depended on a faithful friend to send him the news of the world. There was thus a whole system of communication, a very profession of letter-writing, which today has changed its nature somewhat and become severed from its personal connection. The nearest modern parallel to the intelligencers who served Anthony Bacon, Essex or the Fuggers is " Our Special Correspondent ". And the influence which a particularly able set of correspondents gave a statesman was comparable to the advantage that a newspaper derives from being " first with the news ".

It was thus no small service that the Bacons were able to render the Earl, and in the stormy waters of Elizabeth's court any aid was welcome. The court was magnificent and dirty, patriotic and torn by the fiercest personal animosities, and the ageing Queen, still deeply susceptible to the charms of lusty young men, had the knowledge and skill to be the ablest diplomat in Europe and was the victim of passions and follies more becoming to a love-torn woman of twenty. There is no doubt about the impression that the affairs of the court made on the members. One of Anthony Bacon's correspondents writes to him while he was still abroad : " There was never at court such emulation, such envy, such back-biting as is now at this time." Spenser, brought over from Ireland by Raleigh, tells the same tale with more circumstance :

And, sooth to say, it is no sort of life
For shepherd fit to lead, in that same place,
Where each one seeks with malice and with strife
To thrust down other into foul disgrace—
Himself to raise ; and he doth soonest rise
That best can handle his deceitful wit
In subtle shifts, and finest sleights devise,
Either by slandering his well-deemed name
Through easings lewd, and feigned forgery ;
Or else by breeding him some blot of blame,
By creeping close into his secrecy ;
To which him needs a guilefull hollow heart,
Washed with fair-dissembling courtesy.

The very history of the favourites of the moment is ample justification of these charges, and shows that to be a courtier was no easy task, and that the velvets and lace, pearls and gold embroidery covered anxious hearts and scheming heads.

In 1582 Raleigh came to court, an ambitious young West Countryman, who had been living a riotous life

as a law student at the Temple and putting in some
fighting in Europe and Ireland. He attempted to
attach himself to the Earl of Leicester, and his letters
are an interesting parallel to those that Bacon wrote
to Burghley. His declarations of devotion are
couched in almost the same words—it was, in fact,
the accepted language of the day.

" If your Lordship shall please to think me yours,
as I am, I will be found as ready, and dare do as much
in your service, as any man you may command."

But Leicester was not responsive. Still Raleigh
was too resourceful to be left long unnoticed and by
1583 was already being talked of as the " new favourite " and by 1586 had become captain of the guard.
This was a decorative position of personal service on
the Queen, and his " guard " were fifty handsome
youths who waited at table and attended functions—a
very good position and one eminently suited to the
favourite of the hour. But Leicester was not to be
ousted thus easily, though he was drawing near his
death. He had in his stepson, Essex, an assistant
who for looks, intelligence and general attractiveness
was Raleigh's equal. So Essex came to court, and
for a while the two men held a precarious equality.
In the ceremonies to celebrate the defeat of the
Armada, delayed somewhat by mourning for Leicester,
Essex was somewhat nearer the Royal Person.

" On this day, being Sunday, attended by her Privy
Council, surrounded by a brilliant concourse of
nobility, with the foreign ambassadors, the judges and
bishops, she made a procession to S. Paul's, seated in
a magnificent chariot throne, raised on four pillars,
and surmounted by a canopy, with an imperial crown
on the top. It was drawn by two milk-white coursers,

and ornamented by a lion and a dragon supporting the arms of England. Around it marched the Queen's footmen and pensioners, after whom came the Earl of Essex leading her horse of state richly caparisoned, followed by the ladies of honour, and on each side the royal guard, commanded by Sir Walter Raleigh, sumptuously apparelled and armed."

In the next year the gossips record that Essex had " cleared Raleigh from the court and confined him in Ireland ". The " clearing " was denied, but Raleigh returned with Spenser in his train (perhaps to add lustre to his state by words as Shakespeare did to Southampton or Bacon to Essex) and the bitterest hostility to his rival in his heart, and while Essex fretted out his short and brilliant day Raleigh sat in his study at Durham House, looking right over the Thames, and planned and despatched his unhappy colonies for Virginia.

There were thus at least two factions, the Cecils and Raleigh, bitterly hostile to Essex, and though he married Walsingham's daughter her powerful father was dead, and Robert Cecil already established in the secretaryship. It was thus a gamble when Francis Bacon threw in his lot with Essex, but a gamble justified by his position. The Cecils would not help him, he seems to have had no dealings with Raleigh, whom nearly all the court regarded as an ill-bred upstart, and he was too plain, sickly, and grave to help himself by his own sex-appeal. So to Essex he turned with such hopes as men have of their patrons—hopes for himself, hopes for the state—and began a period of service which was honourable because honest.

CHAPTER IV

THE CANVASS FOR OFFICE

AT first the Bacon-Essex alliance did well. Essex was appointed privy councillor, rose in reputation and in 1594 was lucky enough to unmask a serious conspiracy against the Queen's life. Francis Bacon improved the occasion by a pamphlet setting out the history of the matter entitled " A True Report of the Detestable Treason Intended by Dr. Roderigo Lopez ". As the whole matter had been unravelled after the Cecils had declared that there was nothing in it, the party at Essex House must have felt that they had scored.

Bacon's pen was in request for other purposes. Part of the duty of a court favourite was to provide her Majesty with amusement, and the taste of the time favoured " devices ", decorative pieces of acting accompanied by elaborate and lengthy speeches. For some of these, presented by Essex, Bacon wrote the words, and put into the mouth of a hermit, a secretary of state, a soldier, discourses of advice on the proper mode of life. They are eloquent and for the most part conventional.

" The gardens of Love where he now playeth himself are fresh today and fading tomorrow, as the Sun comforts them or is turned from them. But the gardens of the Muses keep the privilege of the golden age ; they ever flourish and are in league with time. The monuments of wit survive the monuments of power; the verses of a poet endure without a syllable lost, while states and empires pass many periods."

Well-recited they would have interested for their phrasing and neat arguments, and if they seem rather an intellectual amusement it must be admitted that the Elizabethans loved a good speech as the modern loves a good piece of back-chat.

From Bacon's own point of view a more important matter was his own advancement. The clear understanding between himself and Essex was that there should be an exchange of benefits, and preferment should follow his devoted attachment. Francis, a lawyer by profession, naturally looked to the law for his support, and it so fell out that at this time the Attorneyship was vacant. Essex at once cast his eye on it for his partisan and an energetic canvass followed which dragged on, hope being even deferred for a year. For this office Bacon was young, being only thirty-three, but there was a far stronger reason for rejecting his claim—he had offended the Queen.

In the parliament of 1593 Bacon sat as Knight of the Shire for Middlesex and was a highly-respected member of the House, being regularly appointed to committees and taking a leading part in debate. He was then, and remained all his life, an enthusiastic parliamentarian, believing in the dignities of the House and holding special views on its relation to the sovereign. On the present occasion he was unfortunate. The Queen seems to have had a scheme for forcing the Lower House to abrogate some of its rights to control finance, by inducing it to join the Lords in a conference to determine the amount

QUEEN ELIZABETH

[*face p.* 40

necessary to meet the needs of the moment. The proposal came as a surprise to the House, but Bacon, with his clear grasp of facts, saw through the proposal and immediately moved its rejection. And after some time spent in debate and confusion, his motion was carried and the government forced to withdraw. Bacon had behaved with strict moderation, but the fact remained that it was largely owing to his quick wit that a constitutional point of great importance had been decided against the government. The Queen was furious, and Bacon, though he protested that he had acted according to his conscience and was deeply grieved to have given offence, could not bring himself to make a submission sufficiently abject to appease his sovereign.

In addition to the Queen's hostility, Bacon was regarded coldly by the court parties. He had endeavoured to keep up with the Cecils, and while he wrote himself to Robert and his half-brother Thomas Cecil, his mother wrote to her brother-in-law, Burghley. The answer returned is as damning in its evasion and faint praise as anything could be.

Good Madam,

I thank you for your kind letter, and for your son's. I think your care of them is no less than they both deserve, being so qualified in learning and virtue as if they had a supply of more health they wanted nothing. But none are, or very few, *ab omni parte beati*; for such are not elect, but subject to temptations from the highway to heaven. For my goodwill to them, though I am of less power to do my friends good than the world thinketh, yet they shall not want the intention to do them good. And so God continue you in his favour by your medications, and that I as your old friend may be partaker of your good wishes and prayers.

From my house at Theobald's, the 29th of August, 1593.
Your Ladyship's loving brother-in-law,
W. Burghley.

Bacon's chief competitor for office was Coke, at that time Solicitor, and his elder by some seven years. Coke had been Speaker of the House of Commons and shown himself a dexterous party man of the government, and if his temper was notoriously savage and his judgment unreliable, he was also known for his learning and his devotion to his profession. Bacon, on the other hand, had never practised in the courts and was now driven, for the sake of his reputation, to do something.

His first appearance seems to have gained favourable notice and his second no less. His arguments were " a *bataille serrée*, as hard to be discovered as conquered. The unusual words wherewith he had spangled his speech were rather gracious for their propriety than strange for their novelty, and like to serve both for occasions to report and means to remember his argument. Certain sentences of his, somewhat obscure, and as it were presuming upon their capacities, will I fear make some of them rather admire than commend him ". In fact, Bacon seems to have been, like the commentator, letting off verbal crackers.

It was all to no good. Coke received the Attorneyship and Bacon, somewhat humiliated, had to start all over again a fresh canvass for the now vacant Solicitorship.

Essex was as deeply engaged in the matter as Bacon, though for a different reason. He was a man who claimed to have his every whim gratified, and the Queen was now refusing him something on which he had set his heart. After one of the usually stormy interviews he wrote to Bacon :

" I have dealt confidently with the Queen, as of a matter wherein I did more labour to overcome her delays than I did fear her denial. I told her how much you were cast down with the correction she had already given you, that she might in that point hold herself already satisfied. . . . I find the Queen very reserved, staying herself from giving any kind of hope, yet not passionate against you till I grew passionate for you. . . . She said she neither was persuaded nor would hear of it till Easter, when she might advise with her council, who were now all absent, and therefore in passion bade me go to bed, if I would talk of nothing else. Wherefore in passion I went away, saying while I was with her I could not but solicit for the cause and the man I so much affected, and therefore I would retire myself till I might be more graciously heard. And so we parted. Tomorrow I will go hence of purpose, and on Thursday I will write an expostulating letter to her. That night or upon Friday morning I will be here again, and follow on the same course, stirring a discontentment in her."

Bacon was still in displeasure and denied access to the Queen, so could not plead for himself. The agonized anxiety that such mad advocacy of his cause must have produced in him can be imagined. Day by day he collected news, pondered omens, wrote letters urging his friends to make a fresh effort or hold their hands for a while and wait till the gale shifted. It was not only the heart-sick misery of waiting for a decision, it was a game of skill where the tools turned in your hands like the flamingo in Alice's game of croquet. It was worse : it was a gamble where every day found Francis and Anthony deeper in debt and with less hopes of meeting their creditors. Anthony was the better endowed of the two brothers and without his

help Francis must have succumbed, taken seriously
to the practice of the law, which he dreaded as it
would have eaten up the time he craved for study,
or become a poor scholar and devoted himself to
learning, setting aside all hope of the power that high
place would confer on him.   But fortunately Anthony
showed a more than brotherly generosity.   Without
complaint or protest, he paid Francis's debts, went
surety for him, helped him to the very limits of his
credit.   It was not only that occasional demands were
made, but accounts show that borrowing went on
continually.   Between September and Christmas, 1593
Francis borrowed £54 in five sums.   In the next year,
between January and September, £260 in six instal-
ments.   These were comparatively petty sums.   The
larger amounts were borrowed to pay off existing
debts, and still the brothers became ever more deeply
involved.   It is an extraordinary testimony to the
strength of their mutual affection, or to their tactful
manners, that the frankness and friendliness of their
relationship was quite unimpaired.

In spite of all this help, Francis began to break down
under the strain.   He wrote to Essex: "I must
confess this very delay hath gone so near me, as it
hath almost overthrown my health."   And even to
the people about him this condition was noticeable.
"I am sorry your brother with inward secret grief
hindereth his health," someone writes to Anthony.
"Everybody saith he looketh thin and pale."

Even more remarkable than this loss of physical
health was that Francis lost his temper.   For perhaps
the single time in his life he wrote a letter in anger.
The strain of keeping up a correspondence with the
Cecils in the tone of a hopeful, devoted suitor was

too much for him. Robert, his equal in age, his inferior in health and ability, was firmly fixed in one of the chief posts under the government. To continue to profess duty, respect and affection to him, when he believed his every word false, was more than he could manage.

" Sir, your Honour knoweth my manner is, though it be not the wisest way, yet taking it for the honestest, to do as Alexander did by his physician, in drinking the medicine and delivering the advertisement of suspicion. So I trust on and yet do not smother what I hear. I do assure you, Sir, that by a wise friend of mine, and not factious towards your Honour, I was told with asseveration that your Honour was bought by Mr. Coventry[1] for two thousand angels, and that you wrought in a contrary spirit to my Lord, your father. And he said farther that from your servants, from my Lady, from some councillors that have observed you in the business, he knew that you wrought underhand against me. The truth of which tale I do not believe. You know the events will show and God will right. But as I reject this report, so I admit a conceit that the last messenger my Lord and yourself used dealt ill with your Honours, and that word (speculation) which was in the Queen's mouth rebounded from him as a commendation, for I am not ignorant of those little arts. Therefore, I pray, trust him not again in my matter. This was much to write, but I think my fortune will set me at liberty, who am weary of asserviling myself to every man's charity."

Whatever the cause—Cecil's hostility, Bacon's youth, his supposed absorption in speculative pursuits

---

[1] A competitor for the post.

to the neglect of the practical, the intemperance of
Essex's methods—Francis was not to have the post.
In November, 1595, two years after the canvass had
started, Sergeant Fleming obtained the Solicitorship,
and there being no more suitable posts available
Bacon settled down to make the best of his life.

One consolation he did receive. Essex, generous
and remorseful at his failure, made Bacon a present
of an estate, which he later " sold for £1,800 to
Master Reynold Nicholas ", and thought was worth
more. Of the manner of the gift Francis speaks with
the warmest gratitude : his own manner of acceptance
indicates a changed relation between the two men.
Bacon had had some four years of the Earl's intimacy.
He had seen his violence, his folly in his dealings with
the Queen, and his furious pursuit of whatever trifle
he set his mind upon. The glorious youth was
growing into the dangerous man, who knew no
principles but his pride. Bacon too was older. He
had become a public man, even if he had failed to
become a public official. He had no immediate
hopes that Essex could serve, and he saw many ways
in which his patron might be dangerous. All this
he put into the words of warning with which he
accepted the gift. " My Lord, I see I must be your
homager, and hold land of your gift, but do you know
the manner of doing homage in law ? Always it is
with a saving of his faith to the King and his other
Lords, and therefore, my Lord, I can be no more
yours than I was, and it must be with the ancient
savings ; and if I grow to be a rich man, you will
give me leave to give it back to some of your un-
rewarded followers."

CHAPTER V

THE DUTIES OF A LEARNED COUNSEL

THE year 1595 brought other changes to Bacon's life beside the definite abandonment of the hope of advancement in his profession. Essex entered on a new phase of his career and that could not fail to affect his friend and follower.

In this year Raleigh had been off on his celebrated voyage to Guiana. He had only received permission to go after many demands, and the voyage itself was not lucky. It could hardly have been so. Raleigh went to find gold, and the coastal districts near the mouth of the Orinoco into which he penetrated do not contain it. The country was unknown, very large, with difficult shifting and torrential rivers, matted forests and inhabitants not always friendly. The band of explorers struggled gallantly with the obstacles of nature, and returned having added a sizable district to the known world. But by Elizabethan standards they had failed and their reception in England was cool. For all that, however, the voyage awakened a fresh burst of enthusiasm for sea adventure, and the very next year saw an expedition ready to sail for Cadiz to repeat the now traditional exploit of singeing the King of Spain's beard. On this expedition Essex was determined to go. Raleigh, as he had just demonstrated his seamanship, could not be excluded. The chief command was divided between the elderly Lord High Admiral, Howard, and Essex. Francis Vere, one of the leading generals of the day, went in command of the troops. An imposing expedition, and one which should have had great results. It got off, however, under difficulties, and Essex, writing to Bacon, gives a very good hint of his perplexities.

" Sir, I have thought the contemplation of the art military harder than the execution. But now I see, where the number is great, compounded of sea and land forces, the most tyrones and almost all voluntaries, the second officers equal almost in age, quality, and standing in the wars, it is hard for any man to approve himself a good commander. So great is my zeal to omit nothing, and so short my sufficiency to perform all, as, besides my charge, myself doth afflict myself. For I cannot follow the precedents of our dissolute armies, and my helpers are a little amazed with me, when they are come from governing a little troop to a great, and from small men to all the greatest spirits of our state. And sometimes I am as much troubled with them as with all the troops."

The troubles with the men extended to the commanders, Raleigh apparently supplying the brains of the party, but being so grievously lacking in tact that only fortune enabled him to get his way. In any case, after a preliminary repulse from the town, the fleet sailed into the harbour, attacked the four great galleons, named after the Apostles, that had been moored to defend the narrows, defeated them, chased all the shipping on shore and then returned to capture and sack the town. The total result was very gratifying, and the Spaniards showed their characteristic lack of decision so that the fleet got away safely. But, as in most other expeditions, the division and total quantity of the booty caused great dissatisfaction, and all the commanders accused each other of spoiling plans which would have resulted in far greater gain.

We can, however, judge that Elizabeth considered the investment profitable on the whole, because the very next year the fleet was off again, this time with Essex in supreme command and Raleigh as a subordinate. However, Fortune did not smile so kindly this time, and Essex, who appears to have been an utterly incompetent commander, kept the fleet sailing about the Azores waiting for the Plate fleet, and then, by complete folly, missed it. Raleigh performed the only exploit of the voyage, and Essex was so enraged by his subordinate's success that he nearly executed him for mutiny on the spot.

These activities not only separated Bacon and Essex in space but also in thought. It was Bacon's considered opinion that Essex would involve himself in serious trouble if he continued in his present manner. A man might be a successful general or admiral and be safe ; but a man who quarrelled openly with the Queen because he was not allowed to dictate to her in the matter of public appointments, who sulked in his chamber for a fortnight till the Queen made a lover-like ending to the dispute, who had managed to win a large party among the common people and boasted of his power, had better content himself with civil offices and not add the suspicion that he could compass armed rebellion to his other failings. Essex thought otherwise, and seemed to claim the power to dictate to Elizabeth as a Queen in the same high-handed way that he dictated to her as a woman. The result was that all real intimacy ceased between the

4

two men, and though letters passed between them, though they met and transacted business, though Bacon every now and then wrote a letter for the Earl in a style that he thought the other ought to adopt, the friendship was gone, and Bacon's influence as a counsellor at an end.

On the other hand, Bacon became more and more engaged in his own business. For some time he had been acting as one of the Queen's Learned Counsel, which meant that he was regularly employed in state cases, and the task which frequently fell to his lot was the interrogation of prisoners. It was customary in those days for the Crown to come into court with what it considered a perfect case, and a part of this was nearly always the prisoner's own confession. This was considered almost essential, and very severe measures, including occasionally torture, were taken to obtain it. The reason was probably twofold. The Crown felt that it had suffered a notable disgrace if one of its prosecutions failed, and the surest way to ensure success was to have the prisoner's own confession. But—and this was the real difficulty—if when in court the prisoner denied his own statement and declared that it had been extracted under torture, the court was very likely to decide in his favour and the government's case was worse than ever. That is the reason why torture was so comparatively rare. In the second place there is much more satisfaction in executing a criminal who confesses than one who resolutely denies the charge, and this feeling is not altogether extinct today. Thus the interrogation of prisoners, especially those accused of political offences, was a task of importance, and in those days one which recurred at short intervals.

Bacon was peculiarly well-suited for the work. He had a mind quick, subtle and patient, and he had a manner that was invariably calm and polite. It would be an ingenious prisoner who evaded his questions, and an unreasonable one who was thrown into obstinacy by an unwise approach. Consequently he was often employed, and thus the two mile walk from Gray's Inn to the Tower must have been one that Bacon took frequently.

The interrogations were held in a room in the Lord Lieutenant's lodgings that has a view across the river. One entered by the main gate, beneath what is now called the Bloody Tower, turned to the left, crossed the small space of garden, and so entered the timbered and gabled house that breaks the fortress monotony of the walls. The prisoner was brought from his cell and found himself confronted by three or four examiners who had before them a list of questions carefully prepared and designed to explore some particular point. A fellow-prisoner, accused of the same crime, had probably been asked the same questions, and there were the examiners, sitting lynx-eyed and quick, ready to detect discrepancies of statement, evasions, or signs of embarrassment.

Not only was there the nervous strain of imprisonment and close questioning, but there was always the threat of torture in the background. No prisoner knew for certain that he would not be subjected to it, nor did he know just how long the patience of his examiners would last. Thus, however calmly Bacon spoke to him, this process of being examined upon interrogatories was a fearsome business.

On certain occasions the examiners used all the rigours at their command. This happened when they

thought that there had been a widespread plot and
they wished to have the names of the confederates.
To procure these they would torture the one person
they had caught. Guy Fawkes, in the next reign,
suffered for this reason, and small mercy would be
shown under Elizabeth to a Jesuit. Father Gerard
was one of the unfortunates, examined before Coke,
Bacon, Waad (the Lieutenant of the Tower) and
others, who refused to give the names of those
concerned in his activities. He was questioned,
threatened, and told that if he did not give way they
would " prolong the torture from day to day as long
as life lasted ".

His own record of what follows reads : " We went
in a sort of solemn procession, the attendants preceding
us with lighted candles because the place was under-
ground and very dark, especially about the entrance.
It was a place of immense extent, and in it were ranged
diverse sorts of racks and other instruments of
torture. Some of these they displayed before me and
told me that I should have to taste them. They led me
to a great upright beam or pillar of wood, which was
one of the supports of this vast crypt."

He was made to stand on a stool and his wrists put
into iron bracelets attached to a beam. The stool was
taken away and he was left to hang. Being a heavy
man, the pain he suffered was soon intense, but he
refused to give any information. The process was
repeated next day, and he was still constant, after
which the examiners decided to leave him alone and
he escaped. But the damage was very severe. For
three weeks his hands were completely paralysed, and
it was five months before the sense of touch returned.
Other men, of less heroic character, needed only the

journey to the vaults and a sight of the manacles to induce them to talk freely.

An unpleasant duty this, but an official must take what work his post brings him. Even in this sensitive age the most humane and genial prison doctor must certify men as duly hanged and stand by to see them flogged. Even so sheltered an official as a school inspector now and then summarily dismisses a headmaster and deprives the drunken wretch of all means of livelihood. The Elizabethans were accustomed to corpses, to heads rotting on London Bridge, or men being flogged through the streets. Interrogating prisoners was not nice, but Bacon and his fellow-examiners were acting with as much consciousness of patriotic duty as a commanding officer who, in war-time, orders a deserter to be shot.

A pleasanter occupation was the publication in 1597 of the first edition of the *Essays*. To one accustomed to the later versions the first set make curious reading. There are only ten of them, all brief, and many of them were greatly extended later. There are none of the most famous, such as the essays on *Death* or *Friendship*. They deal with Study, Discourse, Ceremonies, Followers and Friends, Suitors, Expense, Regiment of Health, Honour, Faction and Negotiating, and they are written as by a man who has had experience of the world and found all bitter. There is not one word of affection in the whole of them. Rather there is a distinct denial of it.

" There is little Friendship in the worlde, and least of all between equals, which was wont to bee magnified. That is, as betweene superior and inferior, whose fortunes may comprehend the one the other."

How utterly he was later to change his mind can be seen from the Essay on Friendship written in 1625 just before his death.

"For a crowd is not company, and Faces are but a gallery of Pictures, and talk is but a Tinckling Cymball, where there is no Love. . . . But we may go further, and affirm most truly that it is a meere and miserable solitude to want true Friends, without which the World is but a wildernesse."

If we want to know Bacon's true thoughts in 1597 we must look to the dedication, which he addresses to Anthony, his "loving and beloved Brother", and after explaining the rather premature publication continues :

"Since these essays would not stay with their master, but would needes travel abroad, I have preferred them to you that are next myself, dedicating them, such as they are, to our love, in the depth whereof (I assure you) I sometimes wish your infirmities translated upon myself."

Bacon had found friendship in his brother, and returned it ; in the world about he had not found it, but only self-seeking, intrigue, and continual disappointment. He saw no real love, and his denial of it in the essays only represents the attitude that was forced upon him by the conditions of political life. He was thirty-seven and had had no success in life ; he had never fallen in love ; he had seen a man that he desired as a friend dash off into a course of life repugnant alike to sense and prudence. This is enough to make any man think ill of the world, and turn to it not his love but his intelligence.

The first edition of the essays, if they have no word of affection, are full of shrewd observation and good advice. The essay on *Discourse* could not be bettered as a conversational guide to the man or woman of the world.

" Some in their discourse desire rather commendation of wit in being able to hold all arguments, than of judgement in discerning what is true, as if it were a praise to know what might be said, and not what should be thought. Some have certain Commonplaces and Theames wherein they are good, and want variety, which kind of poverty is for the most part tedious and now and then ridiculous.

" The honourable part of talk is to guide the occasion, and again to moderate and pass to somewhat else.

" It is good to varie and mix speech of the present occasion with argument, tales with reasons, asking of questions with telling of opinions, and jest with earnest.

" But some things are privileged from jest, namely Religion, matters of state, great persons, any man's present business of importance, and any case that deserves pity.

" He that questioneth much shall learn much, and content much, especially if he apply his questions to the skill of the person of whom he asketh, for he shall give them occasion to please themselves in speaking, and himself shall continually gather knowledge.

" If you dissemble sometimes your knowledge of that you are thought to know, you shall be thought another time to know that you know not.

" Speech of a man's self is not good often, and there is but one case wherein a man may commend himself with good grace, and that is in commending virtue in another, especially if it be such a virtue as whereunto himself pretendeth.

" Discretion of speech is more than eloquence, and to speak agreeably to him with whom we deal is more than to speak in good words or in good order.

" A good continued speech without a good speech of interlocution showeth slowness ; and a good reply or second speech, without a good set speech, showeth shallowness and weakness, as we see in beasts that those that are weakest in the course are yet nimblest in the turn.

" To use many circumstances ere one come to the matter is wearisome, to use none at all is blunt."

It is a curious picture of Bacon that looks out of this essay, but one which could be very delightful if affection and excitement carried him away from his analysis. It is hard to say if it ever did.

CHAPTER VI

THE TRAGEDY OF ESSEX

IN 1598 Essex had his worst quarrel with the Queen. The question of the Lord Lieutenant of Ireland was under discussion and Essex was urgent for the appointment of Sir George Carew, not on any grounds of public policy, but because having quarrelled with him he wished him removed as far as possible from the court. Essex, on failing of his purpose, turned his back on the Queen with the maximum of rudeness, whereupon she lost her temper and smacked his face, and he put his hand on his sword and swore that he would not stand such treatment from anyone, not Henry VIII himself. This happened in June or July and the rupture continued till October, when it was necessary to send an army to Ireland, and Essex allowed himself to be pacified probably on the understanding that he should have the chief command. But all did not go smoothly, though no one opposed his candidature. First one difficulty occurred to Essex and he must have that righted, and then another, so that it was only in April, 1599, that he finally got away, with an unusually large army, and most unprecedented powers, and the title of Lord Deputy of Ireland.

It should have been a triumphant departure, but those who were in the know regarded the whole matter with grave doubt. A friend wrote to Sir John Harrington :

" I hear you are to go to Ireland with the Lieutenant Essex. If so, mark my counsel. . . . Observe the man who commandeth, and yet is commanded himself : he goeth not forth to serve the Queen's realm, but to humour his own revenge. If the Lord Deputy performs in the field what he hath promised in the Council, all will be well ; but though the Queen hath granted forgiveness for his late demeanour in her presence, we know not what to think hereof. She hath in all outward semblance placed confidence in the man who so lately sought other treatment at her hands. We do sometime think one way and sometime another. You have now a secret from one that wisheth you all welfare and honour. I know there are overlookers set on you all, so God direct your discretion. Sir William Knolles is not well-pleased, the Queen is not well-pleased, the Lord Deputy may be pleased now, but I sore fear what may happen hereafter."

Bacon undoubtedly felt the same, and his letter to Essex on his departure is a carefully-studied warning. The letter is formal and shows that all real intimacy between the two men was at an end, while the elaborate anticipations of success are mingled with the clearest rebukes and exhortations.

" Your Lordship is designed to a service of great merit and great peril, and as the greatness of the peril must needs include a like proportion of merit, so the greatness of the merit may include no small consequence of peril, if it be not temperately governed. For all immoderate success extinguisheth merit and stirreth up distaste and envy, the assured forerunners of whole charges of peril. . . . Therefore I will only add this wish—that your Lordship in this whole action, looking forward, would set down this position, that merit is worthier than fame, and looking back hither, would remember this text, that obedience is better than sacrifice."

To warn Essex so explicitly against an over-weaning ambition, and to fear that his earliest sin is likely to be disobedience, showed a very just appreciation of his character.

On the other hand, Essex's supporters set to work to organize popular opinion in his favour. There were no newspapers, and the stage was probably the most powerful organ of the day, and Shakespeare was the most popular playwright. Through Southampton, Essex had a claim on his verse, and the play, *Henry V*, which appeared at this time spoke in no uncertain tongue :

> . . . Now we bear the King
> Towards Calais. . . .
> Behold the English beach
> Pales in the flood with men, with wives and boys,
> Whose shouts and claps outvoice the deep-mouthed sea,
> Which, like a mighty whiffler, 'fore the King,
> Seems to prepare his way : so let him land,
> And solemnly see him set on to London.
> So swift a pace hath thought that even now
> You may imagine him upon Blackheath ;
> . . . But now behold,
> In the quick forge and working house of thought
> How London doth pour out her citizens.
> The mayor and all his brethren in best sort
> Go forth and fetch their conquering Caesar in :
> As, by a lower, but by loving likelihood,
> Were now the general of our gracious empress
> As in good time he may, from Ireland coming,
> Bringing rebellion broached on his sword,
> How many would the peaceful city quit
> To welcome him.

One can well imagine that the actor, having declaimed, waited for the responsive cheers.

But in this same play there is a passage that thrilled as certainly to the hearts of the audience as references to a " woman's honour " touched the minds of the late Victorians. It is the great denunciation of the traitors in Act II beginning :

> But O !
> What shall I say to thee, Lord Scroop ? Thou cruel,
> Ingrateful, savage and inhuman creature.

And reaching its climax with :

> Murder and Treason ever kept together,
> As two yoke-devils sworn to either's purpose.
> And what so ever cunning fiend it was
> That wrought upon thee so preposterously
> Hath got the voice in Hell for excellence. . . .
> I will weep for thee :
> For this revolt of thine, methinks, is like
> Another fall of man.

Elizabethan England had no use for traitors. It was a state permanently at war and therefore had, in many things, a war mentality. It was an age when kings were by God appointed, and literally held the safety of their kingdoms in their hands. A man had many temptations to be false to his monarch. There were quarrels within and bribes without, and treason was a common crime. In our days a traitor is a rare creature, and the one that has been hung in recent years has almost assumed the halo of a martyr; but traitors in Elizabeth's day were common and were hated with a deep, fanatical fury. If a man fell into that category, there was little help for him.

Essex in Ireland did little to justify Shakespeare's predictions of success. His avowed intent was to make an attack on Tyrone, the leader of the rebels, in Ulster. But he did not do so. He wasted the campaigning season in skirmishes farther south, and only in the first week of September met Tyrone. Then, instead of fighting with him, he concluded a truce and dashed off home to England, contrary to orders, to lay the matter before the Queen in person.

The Queen was completely in the dark as to the motives of Essex's actions. No one at the time knew what he had really been doing, and even today the whole matter is uncertain. There is every probability that he had been corresponding with James as to his succession to the English throne. This of course was forbidden. Elizabeth did not like to contemplate either her successor or her death, and although she was ageing tried to cheat time by denying him. Still to correspond with the man generally accepted as the next king of the country was not a very unnatural or immoral thing to do, and Cecil from the shelter of his official position did it extensively. But there is a chance that the crimes went deeper, and that Essex contemplated invading England with his Irish army, possibly augmented with some of Tyrone's ruffians. If he did, that slap the Queen gave him had turned his head.

There is about his conduct from now till his death a madness which suggests the old idea that *Quem Deus vult perdere, prius dementat*. The Greeks had noticed the madness that comes upon the doomed, and Essex seems to have joined their number and to be realizing all Bacon's forebodings.

The Queen received Essex mildly and did nothing worse than confine him, in charge of his friend the Lord Keeper, at York House. The complaint she had against him was merely his ill success in Ireland and the fact that he had left his charge contrary to orders. After some discussion, and contrary to Bacon's advice, she decided to have a statement made in the Star Chamber on the matter, in the hope that this official announcement would quiet the popular feeling on his behalf. For the propaganda in his favour had been successful, and Essex was something of a popular hero.

But this course was unsuccessful. The people, hearing the charge but not Essex's defence, thought that deep malice underlay the matter, and feeling was as hot as ever. So finally a special court was formed of the Council which met at the Lord Keeper's house, and there Essex had to answer the charges against him. The Queen's Learned Counsel, including Bacon and Coke, had to present the case, and the intended procedure was that Essex should admit the charges and humbly ask for pardon, which in due course should be given him. The plan nearly miscarried because Coke dealt with the charge in such an irritating way that Essex was tempted to justify himself, but after the court had interposed the matter went off as arranged and the president passed sentence— "that he should be suspended from the execution of his offices and continue in his own house until it should please Her Majesty to release both this and all the rest ".

To this trial some two hundred members of the public were admitted, and as they were men of diverse professions and walks of life the government trusted that they would give an account which would put an end to the gossip and ill-feeling.

This was at least partially accomplished, and the Queen, having exacted her submission, set Essex free at the end of a month and after six weeks gave him complete liberty, save that he must avoid the court. For the time at least the paths of ambition were closed to him, but all else was open, yet there is reason to think that the Earl regarded the status of a private man, however rich or well born, as but " misery " and was ready rather to die than endure it.

Of his return to favour there was even a hope. Bacon urged it, and found that to plead the Earl's case put him on rather good terms with the Queen. He even took the trouble to draft letters which he thought would be suitable for Essex to write, and then saw to it that the letters fell into the Queen's hands !

These ingenious devices might have borne fruit had Essex waited a little. But he did not. While he was still a prisoner, he had started on some plot in conjunction with Southampton and others, and now this plot was revived. It was directed in the first place, it seems, against Sir Walter Raleigh, and some other court enemies, whose influence he felt was being used against him. These were almost certainly to be killed. After that, when they had forced their way to the Queen's presence, something was to occur, but as testimony conflicts and as the matter never came to actions, we cannot say what it was. There is about this plot an incredibly silly air ; so silly that one almost wonders if the Earl had not been entrapped into it by someone who was determined on his ruin. Raleigh probably fell a victim to the machinations of Robert Cecil and Howard ; it is possible that an *agent provocateur* suggested the farcical proceeding by which Essex lost his life. Southampton at his trial asserted firmly that it was " ignorance of the law " that had destroyed him, but no man could have been ignorant that to attack the court with armed forces was a crime. Whatever the true reason, this is what seems to have happened.

At Michaelmas, 1600, the patent that Essex held for sweet wines expired, and he had persuaded himself that its renewal was a test of the Queen's intentions towards him. By October all hope of it was gone and he plunged into intrigue. By February 7th the conspirators were nearly ready. To hearten themselves for the adventure they had sent over to Shakespeare's company and asked for a performance of *Richard II*. To the reply that it was an old play that would no longer draw, they replied by a gift of money roughly equivalent to buying up the stalls. Strengthened by this ill-omened play, they went on with their preparations. When the stir about Essex's house was so great that the court began to take notice, a curious meeting took place on the river. Sir Walter Raleigh sent to Sir Fernando Gorges, one of the conspirators, to come to Durham House to speak with him. Essex, hearing of the proposal, insisted that the meeting must be by water. This is the account that Sir Fernando gave subsequently :—

" When Sir Walter Raleigh's boat came to me, he being all alone and I having two gentlemen, he told me that he had sent for me to admonish me to make all haste out of the town, there being a warrant out for the sending me to the Fleet. For his kind advertisement I gave him thanks, but told him withal, because I knew the present occasion would soon discover itself, that it came too late, for I had engaged myself in another matter. He farther enquired of me what it was. I told him there were two thousand gentlemen who had resolved that day to live or die free men. He protested unto me he heard not of it until that morning, but did not see what they were able to do against the Queen's authority. My answer was, it was the abuse of that by him and others which made honest men resolve to seek a reformation thereof."

So they parted. But because Gorges would not use his superiority of numbers to kill or capture Raleigh, Blount sent four shots after the departing boat, and fortunately missed.

All this suggests the clearest premeditation, and if *Richard II* can be taken as presaging their true intents, they were all guilty of treason in the highest degree.

These facts being well known to the court, the Lord Keeper and three others of the Lords, all friends of Essex, came down to his house to ask what was happening and promising to report any grievances to the Queen. They were admitted to the house and then kept prisoner, an act further highly treasonable. Then, on foot, for the horses were not ready, a little band, with Essex leading, set out for the City and tried to rouse the people on the cry that the Earl was in danger and the country sold to Spain. So all along Cheapside and Gracechurch Street to the house of Sheriff Smith, who, like a wise man, would have none of it and withdrew to consult the Lord Mayor. The Lord Mayor did nothing, and Essex must set off home again. The land side was beset, so he took boat and arrived by water. By ten o'clock that night the house had been invaded, the defenders had surrendered and all were removed to prison.

Inquiries immediately followed. Bacon was working at his old task of examining prisoners, and fairly soon enough of the matter came out to make a public trial possible. The indictment was divided up as before, and it is curious to notice how closely this trial follows the outlines of the previous one, save only in the fact that Essex was now too proud or too desperate to go through even a decent ritual of penitence. This trial is one of the most remarkable and ill-managed in the history of English law. Too much importance must not be attributed to the actual trial. There was no doubt at all as to what Essex had done, and there was also no doubt, though the Lords heard legal evidence on the matter, that those deeds constituted treason. From this the sentence followed automatically. But there was never the slightest chance that the sentence of the court would be carried out. Gentlemen of the rank of Essex and Southampton were not drawn on a hurdle through the streets, nor submitted to the bloody horrors of a common death. There was every possibility that they would both escape punishment altogether. Southampton, who was charged and condemned equally with Essex, was reprieved at once and continued his turbulent life for many years. Essex would in all probability have escaped also if he could but have brought himself to make a speech of proper humility after hearing the judgment of the court. Elizabeth demanded a supple bearing from her servants, and as Bacon had suffered for not apologizing for a speech in Parliament, so Essex probably went to his death because he would not throw himself on her Royal grace, but preferred to ask for a clergyman and protest his steadfastness in the true religion. In any case life and death lay with the Queen—such open rebellion could not go unnoted—and the court proceedings were as nearly formal as possible. The judgment of the court, which was inevitable, merely meant that the Queen could legally execute the two Earls if, after consideration and due observance of their behaviour, she thought it desirable.

The report of the state trial opens with a solid magnificence of description.

" A spacious court was made in Westminster Hall, where the Lord Treasurer Buckhurst sat as High Steward of England, under a canopy of state, where sat also about the table the earls, barons and judges of the land, according to their degrees.

" These sat all in the court next the bar, before the High Steward ; seven sergeants at arms came in with maces before the High Steward, and laid them down before him in the court. The King at Arms stood on the one side of the High Steward by his chair of estate, and one of her Majesty's gentlemen ushers with his white rod in his hand on the other side. The Captain of the Guard (Sir Walter Raleigh) and fourty of the queen's guard were there to attend the service. Then the Sergeant at Arms made three O-yes ! and proclamation. ' That the Lord High Steward of England commanded silence, and to hear the commission read, upon pain of imprisonment.' Then the Clerk of the Crown read the commission, whereunto the Earl of Essex was very attentive . . .

" Then the Lord High Constable of the Tower, the Lieutenant of the Tower, and the gentleman porter, who carried the ax, before the prisoners, came in, and the prisoners followed and made their appearance at the bar, the gentleman porter with the ax standing before them, with the ax's edge from them, and so the Lieutenant delivered his precept into the court. The two Earls (which were prisoners) kissed one another's hands, and embraced each other . . .

" Then they were called to hold up their hands at the bar, which they did. And then the Clerk of the Crown read the Indictments. That being done, they were bid to hold up their hands again, which they did, and another indictment was read, whereunto the Earl of Essex was attentive. After which, the Clerk of the Crown asked them whether they were guilty or not guilty : they pleaded not guilty : and for their trials they put themselves upon God and their Peers. They spake this severally."

The case was opened by Sergeant Yelverton on the point of law. " That if any man do but intend the Death of the King, it is death by the Law : for he is the head of the Commonwealth, and all his subjects as members ought to obey and stand with him."

He was followed by the attorney general, Sir Edward Coke, who, having announced his purpose : " (1) I will open the quality of the rebellion ; (2) the manner of it ; (3) I will touch the circumstances and lastly I will observe the person," made a violent speech to which Essex promptly objected.

Essex : " Will your lordships give us our turns to speak, for he playeth the orator, and abuseth your lordships' ears and us with slanders, but they are but fashions of orators in corrupt states."

This permission was given and very soon Coke and Essex were engaged in acrimonious back-chat of which the following is a sample.

Essex : " Well, Mr. Attorney, I thank God you are not my judge this day—you are so uncharitable."

Attorney General : " Well, my Lord, we shall prove

you anon what you are, which your pride of heart and aspiring mind hath brought you unto."

Essex : " Ah, Mr. Attorney, lay your hand upon your heart and pray to God to forgive us both."

At this point Raleigh intervened to say that he had heard from Fernando Gorges on the water that Essex had fortified his house, and thus provoked another altercation between the two prisoners and Yelverton and Coke. This was calmed while the serious business of the trial proceeded, the reading of the depositions of those who had taken part in or witnessed the rising. The evidence was quite conclusive, and Southampton and Essex made no attempt to refute it. They only urged that when they had reached her Majesty, by whatever means, they would have proceeded " by petition, prostrating ourselves at her Majesty's feet, to have put ourselves unto her mercy." That being future could be neither proved nor denied. For the present action Essex could only plead his personal enemies, whom he names as Cobham, Cecil and Raleigh, and a fear for his life. Even this he does not prove, and the rest of the trial became a disgraceful personal wrangle between the prisoners and Cobham and Cecil. Raleigh, having said his say, remained quiet.

Twice Bacon intervened and attempted to bring the matter to an end. He had probably been charged with the duty of making the concluding speech, and he was trying to do it on both occasions. The two speeches are so similar, both in form and in matter, that they were clearly intended to serve the same final purpose. But the first was ineffective—the wrangle broke out again, this time with a glance at Bacon, and the summing-up had to be done a second time. As final speeches for the prosecution, they are brief and moderate, and the place of personal attack is taken by academic parallels from history. The first speech, and the one Bacon probably prepared, compares Essex to Pisistratus, very much in the manner of a college composition ; the second one makes the more damning comparison to Guise on the Day of Barricades, but French events were new in men's minds and it is a comparison that would spring readily to the lips of a man speaking *extempore*.

The second speech was successful. Essex gave up his semblance of a defence : " My lord, I must confess it was my fault to stand out and to maintain my house with defence and resisting. . . . All which I thought good to remember, and so humbly to submit the same to her Majesty's gracious pleasure."

The court could then proceed to deliver its verdict. The prisoners were withdrawn, the court retired. " After half-an-hour they came all out again, and each man took his place, which being done, the sergeant at arms began with the puisne lord, and called Thomas Lord Howard, who stood up bareheaded.

" *L. Steward* : ' My Lord Thomas Howard, whether is Robert Earl of Essex guilty of this Treason whereupon he hath been indicted, as you take it upon your honour, or no ? '

" Whereupon the Lord Thomas Howard made answer, bending his body, and laying his left hand upon his right side, said : ' Guilty, my lord, of High Treason.' After which manner all the peers found him guilty one after another, from the puisne to the highest, and so delivered in like sort upon their honours. Being called over anew, they found Henry Earl of Southampton guilty of high treason also."

The speeches of the prisoners before sentence was passed on them were of importance, as they probably influenced their fate. Southampton's is in the normal form, admitting his mistake—he admitted nothing worse—and ending : " Since the law hath cast me, I do submit myself to death, and yet I will not despair of her Majesty's mercy, for that I know she is merciful, and if she please to extend it, I shall with all humility receive."

Essex made no mention of mercy in his first speech and, having been prompted thereto in no doubtful terms by the Lord Steward, could get no nearer humility than this :

" My lord, you have made an honourable motion : do but send to me at the time of my death, and you shall see how penitent and humble I will be towards her Majesty. . . . If I had ever perceived any of my followers to have harboured an evil thought against her Majesty, I would have been the first that should have punished the same, in being his executioner ; and therefore I beseech you, my good lord, mistake me not, nor think me so proud that I will not crave her Majesty's mercy, for I protest (kneeling upon the very knee of my heart) I do crave her Majesty's mercy with all humility, yet I had rather die than live in misery."

The formal sentence of the court, which neither was, nor could have ever been meant to be carried out, ran as follows :

" You must go to the place from whence you came, and there remain during her Majesty's pleasure ; from thence to be drawn on a hurdle through London streets and so to the place of execution, where you shall be hanged, bowelled and quartered, your head and quarters to be disposed of at her Majesty's pleasure, and so God have mercy on your souls."

The interest was now fully transferred to the Queen, but she did not relent. After the first proceedings she had gained a victory, as Bacon took the trouble to point out, " over two things, which the greatest princes in the world cannot at their wills subdue : the one is over fame, the other is over a great mind ". At the second trial she had probably failed of both. Popular favour was still on the side of Essex, and has remained there perhaps to the present day, and Essex himself having dared her at the trial to kill him and having asserted that he only cared for life on his own terms, was not a creditable victory.

Even if the Queen had been favourable, the forces of court intrigue were strong against him. Robert Cecil, after the imputations made against him in court, could only wish his death, Raleigh hated him, and there exists a letter which Raleigh wrote in reply to one from Cecil asking his opinion on the Earl's execution.

SIR,

I am not wise enough to give you advice, but if you take it for a good counsel to relent towards this tyrant, you will repent when it shall be too late. His malice is fixed, and will not evaporate by any of your mild courses ; for he will ascribe the alteration to her Majesty's pusillanimity and not to your good nature. The less you make him, the less he shall be able to harm you and yours. Lose not your advantage ; if you do, I read your destiny. Let the Queen hold Bothwell ; while she hath him, he will ever be the canker of her estate and safety. Princes are lost by security and preserved by prevention. I have seen the last of her good days, and all ours, after his liberty.

Yours,

W.R.

With such forces against him, the Earl might well prepare for death.

The Earl's last appearance was on February 25th, 1601, when he passed from the Tower, still called after him, to the church of *S. Peter ad vincula*, and thence, after hearing service, to the scaffold on Tower Green. He was the only man actually executed inside the Tower, and this special regulation was probably due to the height of public feeling. Raleigh was present as captain of the guard, and by one of the strange reversals of fortune, which were commonly happening in those days, he harped back to this very scene when he himself stood on the scaffold.

" It is said that I was a prosecutor of the death of the Earl of Essex, and stood in a window over against him when he suffered, and puffed out tobacco in disdain of him. But I take God to witness that I had no hand in his blood, and was none of those that procured his death. My Lord of Essex did not see my face at the time of his death, for I had retired far off into the armoury, where I indeed saw him, and shed tears for him ; but he saw not me. I will further say that my soul hath many times grieved that I was not nearer to him when he suffered, because as I understood afterwards he asked for me at his death, and desired to have been reconciled to me."

It is pleasing to know that the Earl's end was not polluted by tobacco smoke. It was certainly very edifying.

CHAPTER VII

GARDENS

With Essex's death romance departed from the Elizabethan age. The Queen was old, though still vigorous, and no other young man caught her eye. The heroes of the Armada had left the seas, and Raleigh, who had yet to mount the scaffold, became for the present a steady parliamentarian and devoted his talents to arguing against a bill for restrictions on types of agriculture.

For Bacon the two years were a time of waiting, though occupied, as were all his moments. His besetting anxiety was money. For several years his difficulties had been increasing, and no way of relief had presented itself. Three years ago Bacon had thought of marrying a rich young widow, Lady Hatton, and Essex had written him a testimonial with which to urge his suit. The letter was addressed to Sir Thomas Cecil, the lady's father.

Sir,

I write this letter from the seaside, ready to go aboard, and leave it with my secretary to be by him delivered to you, whensoever he shall know that my dear and worthy friend, Mr. Francis Bacon, is a suitor to my Lady Hatton, your daughter. What his virtues and excellent parts are, you are not ignorant. What advantages you may give both to yourself and to your house by having a son-in-law so qualified, and so likely to rise in his profession, you may easily judge. Therefore to warrant my moving of you to incline favourably to his suit, I will only add this, that if she were my sister or daughter I protest I would as confidently resolve myself to farther it as now I persuade you.

And though my love to him be exceedingly great, yet is my judgment nothing partial, for he that knows him so well as I do cannot but be so affected. In this farewell of mine I pray you receive the kindest wishes of

> Your most affectionate and assured friend,
>
>   ESSEX.

But this recommendation, handsome though it was, and touching in the light of later events, failed to move Lady Hatton, or else Bacon decided at the last minute to face his difficulties alone, for next year the lady married Coke, and brought him her riches and her violent temper. It is hard to say what difference it would have made if Bacon in early middle life had become a relation by marriage of the Cecils and had behind him a private income ample for his needs. On the other hand, Lady Hatton would probably have ruined his chances of domestic peace, so perhaps Coke did not gain so very much by his victory.

However, Bacon suffered immediately. In 1598 he was arrested for debt by one Sympson, a goldsmith, and conveyed to a sponging house. His indignation at the event is partly personal, partly due to a feeling that the Queen's government has been outraged in his person ; and his letters of protest are addressed to no less personages than Sir Thomas Edgerton, Keeper of the Great Seal, and Sir Robert Cecil, Secretary of State. Bacon, if he was in low financial water, was one of the governing class, and could make his complaints heard by the supreme officials of the state. To Edgerton he writes :

" This Lombard having me in bond for £300 principal, and I having the last term confessed the action, and by his full and direct consent respited the satisfaction till the beginning of this term to come, without ever giving me warning by letter or message,

served an execution upon me, having trained me at
such time as I came from the Tower, where, Mr. Waad
can witness, we attended a service of no mean importance. . . . He would have urged it to have had
me in prison, which he had done, had not Sheriff
More, to whom I sent, gently recommended me to an
handsome house in Coleman Street, where I am. . . .
I have an hundred pounds lying by me, which he may
have, and the rest upon some reasonable time and
security ; or if need be the whole, but with my more
trouble. As for the contempt he hath offered, in
regard her Majesty's service, to my understanding,
carrieth a privilege *eundo et redeundo* in meaner causes,
much more in matters of this nature, especially in
persons known to be qualified with that place and
employment."

The first real relief came when Bacon received his
share of the very large fines paid as ransom by those
who had been implicated in the Essex conspiracy and
escaped with their lives. From their ransom Bacon
received £1,200, and this went some distance to
paying his outstanding debts. Moreover, in 1601,
Anthony Bacon died, and though comment of the day
said that he was " so far in debt that I think his brother
is little the better by him ", Francis certainly begins
to settle with his most important creditors.

In the next year he was trying to be free of Mr.
Trott, a creditor who had long been complaisant, but
now grew troublesome, especially in regard to his
rate of interest. Bacon does not seem to have kept
proper records of the separate transactions, and the
dispute became so fierce that it was referred to the
Lord Treasurer. From Bacon's account, drawn up
" as far as he could collect it by such remembrances

as he could find ", he had borrowed £2,650 from
Trott, paid back to him by way of principal and
interest £2,093, and was prepared to pay a farther
£1,259 12s. to get back the mortgage on his favourite
estate of Twickenham Park. It seems probable that
the award of the arbitrators was a little higher than
Bacon's offer, and that on January 22nd, 1602, Bacon
paid the money, redeemed Twickenham Park, and
started his forty-second year a comparatively free
man.

With this problem ever in his mind, it is not strange
if it appears also in his Essays. In the first edition
there is an essay on *Expense*, and this expresses very
well the principles on which he and his brother had
always acted.

" Riches are for spending, and spending for honour
and good occasions. Therefore extraordinary expenditure must be limited by the worth of the occasion,
for voluntary undoing may be as well for a man's
country as for the kingdom of heaven."

Anthony had undoubtedly expended a large part of
his private fortune on organizing his service of
intelligencers, and Francis approved the practice.
Francis on his part had attended court, and on the
occasions of festivals had given the Queen presents
far beyond his means. With this Anthony had
sympathized, and so practically that it had largely been
his resources that supplied the money. The brothers
had been at one in these matters, and their expenses,
embarked on for sound public reasons, were not
extravagance in the ordinary sense of the word.
There is little doubt that in the time of his greatness
Francis Bacon was a careless and somewhat prodigal
master. In his youth and poverty he had a very

just appreciation of the problem, even if he failed to solve it.

Through all these years Bacon continued to reside in Gray's Inn. He went for holidays to Gorhambury or Twickenham Park, but the Inn was his London place of residence and there he spent most of his time. To the affairs of the Inn he devoted much attention. On two occasions he was Reader and delivered a course of lectures and involved himself in the expenses of the office. The second time was in the Lent Vacation of 1600 and the subject chosen was the *Statute of Uses*. Bacon had appeared six years earlier in Chudleigh's case and had then first attracted notice by his manner in court. In this case he had been on the same side as Coke, who included the case in his reports. The reading on the statute was a six days' course. On each day Bacon would deliver a preliminary discourse, take a division of the statute, and finish with a few cases for exercise and argument. The language would probably be Law French, since that was the custom of the Inn, and the discussion such as has been already described.

He had other and lighter occupations in connection with the Inn. During these years he was superintending the laying-out of the garden which became such a fashionable place of resort in the next century. Both Lincoln's Inn and Gray's Inn had a space of open country adjoining them. It was rough land, and the name by which it was called—Coney Garth— suggests tufts of thorn trees and rough banks full of burrows. Lincoln's Inn reclaimed their land, and Bacon made his field a garden. The open country was close at hand and from the lawns and shaded walks of Gray's Inn garden one looked over fields

and hedges to the village of Hampstead. We have
an account for the plants Bacon bought and notes of
the money spent on them :

"71 elm-trees at 9d. each.
8 birch-trees at 1/6 each.
16 cherry-trees at 1/– each."

For several plants of woodbine and eglantine he paid
8/– and 37/– respectively.

"125 standards of roses 12/6
Pincks, violetts and primroses 7/–
Cuttings of vynes 12/6
Laying out walks and gardens £100
Seats £6 13 4."

There was also a mound with a summer-house on
the top.

Broad-sheets of the next century are full of these
gardens and they were a well-known haunt of lovers.
It is pleasant to think that it was under Bacon's
regularly-planted elm-trees that fashion and rascality
mingled.

Money in Elizabeth's day was worth about ten
times as much as it is today. It is clear, therefore, that
the garden, as Bacon planted it, was an expensive
affair. But for this there is justification.

Gardens played a very important part in Elizabethan
life and were esteemed both for themselves and for
their produce. Foreigners to England were struck
by the sweetness of the houses with their rushes, great
bowls of flowers and green leaves for decoration.
The merchant in his office had a jar of carnations
beside him on his desk, and the housewife set her vase
of flowers in the room window to catch the light and
shed fragrance. Herrick has a poem of the sequence
of flowers and leaves in the house for decoration.

Down with the Rosemary and Bayes,
Down with the Miselto ;
Instead of Holly now upraise
The Greener Box (for show).

The Holly hitherto did sway ;
Let Box now domineere ;
Untill the dancing Easter day,
Or Easter's Eve appeare.

Then youthful Box which now hath grace,
Your houses to renew ;
Grown old, surrender must his place,
Unto the crisped yew.

When yew is out then Birch comes in,
And many a flower beside ;
Both of a fresh and fragrant kinde
To honour Whitsontide.

Greed rushes then and sweetest Bents,
With cooler oken boughs ;
Come in for comley ornaments,
To re-adorn the house.

Besides decoration, the garden provided medicine. The prescriptions of the day were mainly herbal and domestic, and the plants grown at home were compounded by the housewife and distributed to her family according to the needs of the moment. This was good for the heart, that for the head, and men of chronic ill-health, such as Bacon, experimented widely with these remedies, and kept notes of their effects, thus building up, each man for himself, a kind of empiric medicine which worked with a certain success.

The value of herbs in actual life meant that there was no sharp distinction, such as there is today, between herbs and flowers. Rosemary, rue, carnations, lavender, mint, savory, marjoram, marigolds are all mentioned together as favours at a feast. But for all that, flower-fanciers, then as now, were eager in the importing and production of new blooms. Some came from overseas. Nicholas Leake, the merchant who had agents in Aleppo, brought in the Martagon lily, the Crown Imperial and the yellow rose of Constantinople. From the East also came the coloured anemones which dominated the minds of gardeners of the period as tulips did later. The heavily-scented carnation—sops in wine—came from Poland. The acacia and lilac were also importations of the day, and Lobel, botanist to James I, produced the lobelia.

Besides these, the gardeners experimented with budding and cross-breeding, and botanical purists were not quite sure that the process was strictly moral.

Perdita : Sir, the year growing ancient,
Not yet on summer's death, nor on the birth
Of trembling winter, the fairest flowers of the season
Are our carnations and streaked gillyvors,
Which some call nature's bastards : of that kind
Our rustic garden's barren, and I care not
To get slips of them.
Polixenes : Wherefore, gentle maiden,
Do you neglect them ?
Perdita : For I have heard it said
There is an art which in their piedness shares
With great creating nature.
Polixenes : Say there be ;
Yet nature is made better by no mean
But nature makes that mean . . .
The art itself is nature. . . .
Perdita : I'll not put
The dibble in earth to set one slip of them ;
No more than, were I painted, I would wish
This youth should say 'twere well, and only therefore
Desire to breed of me.

These were, of course, country prejudices, and the experts of the town conducted their experiments and

6

raised their little plants, and guarded them more carefully than if they had been Orient pearls.

The poets, however, were on the whole faithful to the more established kinds. Sops-in-wine, probably because of their lovely name, were often mentioned, but for the rest lilies, violets and irises, with daffodils, were the chief members of the catalogues that were so common in verse. To the Elizabethan these lists of flowers were natural and beautiful. The words remain to us, but the reality has departed. We no longer strew our roads with blossoms—tar has replaced them. We no longer, after we cease to be children, wear our necklets of daisies or play with cowslip balls. Garlands for the hair are out of fashion, but to the Elizabethan reader the names must have brought vivid images of cool stalks and blossoms and sweet scents and play in gardens and fields.

> Bring hither the pinke and purple columbine,
> With gilliflowers :
> Bring coronations and sops-in-wine,
> Worne of paramoures.
> Strowe me the ground with daffadowndillies,
> And cowslips and kingcups and loved lillies :
> The pretie pawnce,
> And the chevisaunce,
> Shall match with the fayre flowre delice.

Besides their own intrinsic charm and fragrance, the flowers were beautified by associations, some holy and some secular. Roses and pinks symbolized divine love, lilies purity, the clover and trefoil the Trinity, and columbine the seven gifts of the Holy Spirit. Rosemary was for remembrance and the bees liked it ; so Sir Thomas More's garden at Chelsea was over-run with it, and where the Beaufort Street trams now grind the bees hummed and the Lord Chancellor meditated. Fairies were particularly fond of thyme, and on it Titania slept many a night. The sweet-briar, which they called eglantine, was dear to man as well as elves, while carnations and irises were both loved of paramours, and were the representatives of very human bliss.

Nor were gardens for flowers alone. There were orchards and beehives, and the gardener thought his work incomplete if he had not birds. Best of all was a nest of nightingales who sang day and night, and performed the useful task of clearing the trees of caterpillars.

The gardener had pleasure for his eye, health for his body, the sweet warbling of birds and the drone of bees for his ear; he must also have scents for his further delighting. The writers of the day compared these wafted odours, now strong on the breeze, now faint, mingled and varied to sweet soft music. They were the perfecting of the garden—its essence. Bacon, when he came to write on gardens, gives an account of the most delightful, which shows how much he cared and how carefully he observed as he walked to and fro. Shakespeare gives the common comparison :—

> That strain again ! It had a dying fall,
> It came o'er my ear like the sweet south
> That breathes upon a bank of violets,
> Stealing and giving odour.

But Bacon wrote no less well, and for once his style gives up something of its austerity to become beauty.

" And because the breath of flowers is far sweeter in the air (whence it comes and goes like the warbling of music) than in the hand, therefore nothing is more fit for delight than to know what be the flowers and plants that do best perfume the air. Roses, damask and red, are fast flowers of their smells, so that you may walk by a whole row of them and find nothing of their sweetness, yea, though it be in a morning's dew. Bays likewise yield no smell as they grow, rosemary little, nor sweet marjoram. That which above all others yields the sweetest smell in the air is the violet, especially the sweet double violet, which comes twice a year—about the middle of April and about Bartholomewtide. Next to that is the musk-rose, then strawberry leaves dying, which yield a most excellent cordial smell, then the flower of the vines—it is a little dust, like the dust of a bent, which grows upon the cluster in the first coming forth ; then sweet briar, then wallflowers, which are very delightful to be set under a parlour or lower chamber window ; then pinks and gilliflowers ; then the flowers of the lime-tree ; then the honeysuckles, so they be somewhat afar off : of bean flowers I speak not, because they are field flowers. But those which perfume the air most delightfully not passed by as the rest, but being trodden upon and crushed, are three : burnet, wild thyme and water-mints. Therefore, you are to set whole alleys of them to have the pleasure when you walk or tread."

The lay-out of a garden was a matter for anxious thought. To Bacon's mind a garden should have three divisions, a lawn flanked by trees, because the sight of well-trimmed grass was incomparably pleasant to the eye, then followed the formal garden hedged round with box or pleached alleys, and beyond was the wilderness where grass and low plants and bushes made a pleasant place of small unexpected charms. On cool days one walked in the close-fenced, sheltered garden ; in summer, when the sun beat too fiercely on the open lawn, one walked under the shelter of the trees. The Elizabethans wore heavy clothes, silks and velvets and furs, summer and winter, so that the sheltering tree was a necessity in a garden used all the year round.

To secure full use of the garden it must be planted with flowers to fit each season. Bacon's loving catalogue gives an idea of the resources of the garden, though there were many more flowers and bushes than he has mentioned.

" There ought to be gardens for all months of the year, in which severally things of beauty may be in season. For December and January and the latter part of November, you must take such things as are green all the winter: holly, ivy, bays, juniper, cypress-trees, yew, pine, apple-trees, fir-trees, rosemary, lavender, periwinkle, the white, the purple and the blue, germander, flags, orange-trees, lemon-trees and myrtle, if they be stoved, and sweet marjoram warm set. Then followeth for the latter part of January and February the mezerion tree which then blossoms, crocus vernus, both the yellow and the grey, primroses, anemones, the early tulip, hyacinthus orientalis, chamaries fistellaria. For March there come violets, especially the single blue, which are the earliest, the yellow daffodil, the daisy, the almond-tree in blossom, the peach-tree in blossom, the cornelian tree in blossom, sweet briar. In April follow the double white violet, the wallflower, the stock gilliflower, the cowslip, flower-de-luces, and lilies of all natures, rosemary flowers, the tulip, the double peony, the pale daffodil, the French honey-suckle, the cherry-tree in blossom, the damson and plum-trees in blossom, the white thorn in leaf, the lilac-tree. In May and June come pinks of all sorts, roses of all kinds, except the musk, which comes later, honeysuckles, strawberries, bugloss, columbine, the French marigold (*Flos Africanus*), cherry-tree in fruit, ribes, figs in fruit, rasps, vine-flowers, lavender in flowers, the sweet satyrian with the white flower, herba muscaria, lilium convallium, the apple-tree in blossom. In July come gilliflowers of all varieties, musk-roses, the lime-tree in blossom, early pears and plums in fruit, gennitings, quodlins. In August come plums of all sorts in fruit, pears, apricots, barberries, filberts, musk-melons, monk's-hood of all colours. In September come grapes, apples, poppies of all colours, peaches, melocotones, nectarines, cornelians, wardens, quinces. In October and the beginning of November come serrices, medlars, bullaces, roses cut, or removed to come late, holly-hocks and such-like. These particulars are for the climate of London, but my meaning is perceived that you may have ver perpetum, as the place affords."

The garden was the special development of the age. The mediæval castle garden was a tiny thing, packed tight within the fortifications and entered by a locked door. The comparative peace of the Renaissance threw open the countryside to the garden. It was still walled, but it was large, open, and not shut in behind a door. Terraces led down to it from the house and there were raised walks as at Penshurst or at Hampton Court, or even a mound with a summer-house at top, as at Gray's Inn, which enabled the

owner to see over the enclosure out to the country
beyond. The formal garden itself was enclosed yet
again from the main garden. In some cases the walls
were clipped box. At Penshurst these great ramparts
of greenery divide the garden into compartments and
would be ideally adapted for amorous eavesdropping.
In other gardens there were pergolas of " carpenter's
work " and over these vines were trained or eglantine,
honeysuckle or clematis. It was necessary that the
very walls of the garden should smell sweet and the
eglantine, vine or honeysuckle were commoner than
the evergreens. Here and there were little arbours
cut, where lovers could sit or statesmen discuss the
affairs of the nation. Within the formal garden were
beds hedged round, often with box, where a pattern
of flowers close-set charmed the eye with its rainbow
colours. The knot garden at Hampton Court is in
the Elizabethan tradition, the effect being quite
different from our modern herbaceous borders with
their bold masses of colour.

These gardens were charming places for love-
making. At night, by moonlight, the nightingales
sang, and all the flowers gave out their scents. Perhaps
the musicians played on the terrace and their music
floated down between the hedges and walks. There
were arbours to sit in and flowery banks. How
pleasantly by day could one wander beside the beds
and talk and laugh, and what opportunities there were
for pretty compliments.

" One of the ladies, who delighted much in mirth,
seeing Philantus behold Camilla so steadfastly, said
unto him : ' Gentleman, what flower do you like
best in all this border ? Here be fair roses, sweet
violets, fragrant primroses ; here be gilliflowers,

carnations, sops-in-wine, sweet johns, and what may either please you for sight or delight you for savour. Loth we are you should have a posie of all, yet willing to give you one, not that which shall look best but such a one as you shall like best.' "

What could Philantus do but bow gallantly and say : " Of all flowers, I love a fair woman."

Bacon, when he wrote of gardens, did not give a full description of the formal enclosed garden, but it is possible to see what he thought it should be like from the description of the setting of the masque which he presented to Somerset on his marriage. The masque was a splendid compliment and cost Bacon some £3,000 to produce, and it was called the *Masque of Flowers*. The elaboration of the setting is characteristic of Bacon. He had a mind at once severely logical and fantastic. He could write or speak in the most perfectly lucid way, each point clearly distinguished and accurately stated, but he loved, in a childlike way, glitter and colour, quaint conceits and elaborate ornament. His garden setting has both the qualities of his mind, the general scheme is simple—in this case traditional—but the details are of a charming elaboration, and the colour and lights, silver unicorns and gold lions, artificial flowers and painted brick, are a childish dream. It was, of course, the taste of the age, but Bacon did it from liking, not convention, and it must have been extremely pretty. To imagine it, we must forget our brilliant electric lights. Today we can dazzle ourselves so easily that for most people the sensation has lost its charm, but Bacon's lights were comparatively dim, and the torches would waver and the flowers glow dully with their hidden candles.

" When the dance ended, the loud music sounded. On the curtains being drawn was seen a garden of a glorious and strange beauty, cast into four quarters with a cross walk and alleys compassing each quarter. In the middle of the cross walk stood a goodly fountain, raised on four columns of silver. On the tops whereof strode four statues of silver which supported a bowl in circuit containing four and twenty foot and was raised from the ground nine feet in height, in the middle whereof, upon scrolls of silver and gold, was placed a globe garnished with four golden mask heads, out of which issued water into the bowl ; above stood a golden neptune, in height three feet, holding in his hand a trident.

" The garden walls were of brick, artificially painted in perspective, all along which were placed fruit trees with artificial leaves and fruits. The garden within the walls was railed about with rails of three foot high, adorned with balusters of silver, between which were placed pedestals beautified with transparent lights of variable colours. Upon the pedestals stood silver columns, upon the tops whereof were personages of gold, lions of gold, and unicorns of silver. Every personage and beast did hold a torch burning that gave light and lustre to the whole fabric.

" Every quarter of the garden was finely hedged about with a low hedge of cypress and juniper, the knots within set with artificial flowers. In the two first quarters were two Pyramids, garnished with gold and silver and glittering with transparent lights resembling carbuncles, sapphires and rubies.

" In every corner of each quarter were great pots of gilliflowers which shadowed certain lights placed behind them and made resplendent and admirable lustre. The two farther quarters were beautified with tulips of diverse colours, and in the middle and in the corners of the said quarters were set great tufts of several kinds of flowers receiving lustre from secret lights placed behind them."

CHAPTER VIII

THE SCOTTISH SOLOMON

JAMES had loomed like a thunderstorm on the horizon for many years before Elizabeth's death. The old Queen had forbidden any communication with him, and had enforced obedience by the strictest measures. Only Cecil, secure in his office, had kept up a correspondence, discussing matters of English policy, the question of Catholic toleration, the position of the Puritans and such-like matters. When the Queen finally died, everything was ready. Those in office might be anxious, men might turn in their beds in the nightmare of a civil war, but, in fact, James was promptly proclaimed and accepted with complete unanimity. " The proclamation was heard with great expectation and silent joy : no great shouting : I think the sorrow for her majesty's departure was so deep in many hearts that they could not suddenly show any great joy ; though it could not be less 'than exceeding great for the succession of so worthy a king. And at night they showed it by bonfires and singing. No tumult : no contradiction : no disorders in the city : every man went about his business as readily, as peaceably, as securely, as though there had been no change, nor any news ever heard of competitors." In fact, London behaved with complete good sense, and an event of first-class historical importance passed off as quietly as if two kingdoms were not being united, and a new dynasty established on the throne.

Bacon had his private hopes and fears as well as his

public anxieties. A few days before the Queen died, when her condition was known to be hopeless, he started writing to his influential friends. They are very discreet letters, make no mention of politics and merely remind the recipient " of the largeness and fullness " of his affections. When the Queen was actually dead he could write more boldly, and to Scotland, urging on the Scotch ministers that he had really been a party, through his brother, in the correspondence of the Earl of Essex, and complimenting them on " the extraordinary sufficiency, dexterity and temper " which they had always shown in the King's business. He even wrote to the King, telling him of his family and past services.

" This royal virtue of access could not of itself (my imperfections considered) have animated me to make oblation of myself immediately to your Majesty, had it not been joined with an habit of like liberty, which I enjoyed with my late dear Sovereign Mistress. And I was not a little encouraged, not only upon a supposal that unto your Majesty's sacred ears (open to the air of all virtues) there might perhaps have come some small breath of the good memory of my father, but also by the particular knowledge of the infinite devotion and incessant endeavours (beyond the strength of his body and the nature of his times) which appeared in my good brother towards your Majesty's service." Thus fathered and thus brothered, he made bold to offer his duty and service.

The effect was merely a regularization of his position of King's Counsel, and whether he expected anything more is uncertain.

Meanwhile, James advanced on London, the head of a band of Scots, welcomed and fêted on the way,

JAMES I

[*face p.* 92

and met by crowds of suitors who trusted more to their personal charm than the persuasive quality of their letters to win them notice.

The exodus from London became so great that the council put a temporary ban on it. One of those who were stayed was Raleigh, though if ever a man needed to plead his own case early it was he. The delay probably cost him his life.

Bacon, at home, immediately turned his mind to affairs of state, and composed a proclamation that he thought it would be expedient for James to issue. There is nothing more characteristic of Bacon than his continual concern with public business. Officially or unofficially, for reward or without, each matter that came up attracted him, held his attention and led to action. Everything he worked at he did well, and this proclamation, called for by no one, probably never used, is as seemly a composition of its kind as could be devised. It was sent off to the Earl of Northumberland as a free gift without concern that his name should be mentioned. " The use of this may be in two sorts : first properly, if your Lordship think convenient to shew the King any such draught ; because the veins and pulses of this state cannot be but best known here ; which if your Lordship should do, then I would desire you to withdraw my name, and only signify that you gave some heads of direction of such a matter to one of whose style and pen you had some opinion. The other collateral : that though your Lordship make no other use of it, yet it is a kind of portraiture of that which I think worthy to be advised by your Lordship to the King, and perhaps more compendious and significant than if I had set them down in articles."

It was not till James was close to London that Bacon met him. The impression was not wholly favourable.

" His speech is swift and cursory, and in the full dialect of his country; and in point of business, short; in point of discourse, large. He affecteth popularity by gracing such as he hath heard to be popular, and not by any fashions of his own. He is thought somewhat general in his favours, and his virtue of access is rather because he is much abroad in press than that he giveth easy audience about serious things. He hasteneth to a mixture of both kingdoms and nations, faster perhaps than policy will conveniently bear. I told your Lordship once before that (methought) his Majesty rather asked counsel of the time past than of the time to come. But it is early yet to ground any settled opinion."

James, besides his hungry followers and his broad accent, was bringing various things with him to London. He was bringing manners and conduct far coarser than had obtained before. His nicknames for his ministers were of the stable, and the correct and respectable Cecil becomes " my little beagle " in his correspondence. When he was at ease and with his favourites, horseplay was his delight and the rising Villiers, when he wished to divert his master, arranged a mock baptism with a pig in his arms. The jest had the more point because the favourite was always being asked to stand godfather to the highborn babies of England.

Villiers was not yet favourite, but James was already plainly addicted to a vice which had not seriously afflicted British royalty since the days of Edward II. Whatever may have been the customs of

Periclean Athens, Renaissance Italy, pre-war Russia
or the Mora Naba, King of all the Mossi, Englishmen
have steadily disliked homosexuality. It was one
thing for Elizabeth to love Leicester or be captivated
by the handsome person of Essex; it was another for
James publicly to dote on Carr's flaxen hair or Villiers'
effeminate graces. Moreover, Elizabeth kept her
own way and counsel. If the favourites crossed her
they felt her wrath, and she never hesitated between
them and the country's good. James saw no
farther than amusing his darling or enriching his
relations.

The portrait of the man is the worst evidence
against him, sensual, silly, intellectual, the face of the
complete ass who is yet a scholar. Had James been
better or worse, he might have managed more wisely.
There is no more bitter result of autocracy than that
Bacon should have had to serve such a master.

Before ever Parliament met England had a sample of
James's character. A plot was hatched, in a curious
way repeating that of Essex and of the same incredible
stupidity. It is possible that this was a mere intrigue
devised by Cecil and others to make a final sweep of
their political enemies. Certainly nothing was done,
and certainly too Cobham and Raleigh, both of whom
had been mentioned at the trial of Essex, were dragged
in. Cecil hated Raleigh, as did nearly everyone else,
and James had been promptly led to do the same. So
with four or five others, Raleigh was apprehended on
the flimsiest evidence and sent to stand his trial at
Winchester, the plague making London unfit for
assemblies.

It is hard to understand the contemporary attitude
to Raleigh, because, being a poet, he has had the last

word. His defence still rings in our ears, and the
blusterings of Coke and the quieter venom of Cecil
are but the bloodstains on the martyr's robe. But to
his own day he was different.

"He was a tall, handsome, and bold man ; but his
naeve was that he was damnable proud. Old Sr.
Robert Harley, of Brampton-Brian Castle (who knew
him), would say 'twas a great question who was the
proudest, Sr. W. or Sr. Thomas Overbury, but the
difference that was, was judged on Sr. Thomas' side."

Sir Thomas also perished unhappily, so pride was
not a fortunate characteristic.

The trial at Winchester was conducted with the
grossest violence by Coke, the Attorney, and the
conviction secured on the testimony of a single
witness, who was certainly perjured, for he swore at
different times statements that were contradictory.
King, Judge, Attorney were at one in demanding the
sentence, and the jury fetched down from Middlesex
gave it as required. The other prisoners were
sentenced in the same way. Then followed a farce,
so cruel and ingenious that it marks its inventor out
as something more than normal, and the pride which
he took in his invention shows that his moral judgment
was as perverted as his ingenuity. Elizabeth might
vacillate, but it was honest doubt. James was
supremely certain.

"The bishop went to the Lord Cobham, and at the
same time the Bishop of Winchester was with Raleigh,
both by express order from the King, as well to
prepare them for their ends as likewise to bring them
to liberal confessions. Markham was told he should
likewise die, but, by secret message from some friends
at court, had still some hope given him.

" Whilst these men were so occupied at Winchester, there was no small doings about them at court for life or death, some pushing at the wheel one way, some another. The lords of the council joined in opinion and advice to the King, now at the beginning of his reign, to show as well examples of mercy as severity, and to gain the title of Clemens as well as Justus ; but some others, led by their private spleen and passions, drew as hard the other way, and Patrick Galloway, in his sermon on Tuesday, preached so hotly against remissness and moderation of justice as if it were one of the seven deadly sins.

" Warrants were signed and sent to Sir Benjamin Tichborne, on Wednesday last, at night, for Markham, Gray and Cobham, who in this order were to take their turns, as yesterday being Friday, about ten of the clock. A fouler day could hardly have been picked out, or fitter for such a tragedy. Markham, being brought to the scaffold, was much dismayed and complained much of his hard hap, to be deluded with hopes and brought to that place unprepared. One might see in his face the very picture of sorrow, but he seemed not to want resolution ; for a napkin being offered by a friend that stood by to cover his face, he threw it away, saying he could look upon death without blushing.

" The sheriff in the meantime was secretly withdrawn by one John Gill, a Scotch groom of the bedchamber, whereupon the execution was stayed, and Markham left upon the scaffold to entertain his own thoughts, which, no doubt, were as melancholy as his countenance was sad and heavy. The sheriff, at his return, told him that since he was so ill prepared he should yet have two hours' respite, so led him from the scaffold, without giving him any more comfort, and locked him in the great hall.

" The Lord Grey, whose turn was next, was led to the scaffold by a troop of the young courtiers, and was supported on both sides by two of his best friends, and coming in this equipage had such gaiety and cheer in his countenance that he seemed a dapper young bridegroom. At his first coming on the scaffold, he fell on his knees, and his preacher made a long prayer to the present purpose, which he seconded himself with one of his own making, which held us in the rain more than half-an-hour, but being come to a full point, the sheriff stayed him and said he had received orders from the King to change the order of the execution, and that the Lord Cobham was to go before him; whereupon he was likewise led away to Prince Arthur's Hall, and his going away seemed more strange to him than his coming hither, for he had no more hope given him than of an hour's respite.

" The Lord Cobham, who was now to play his part, and by his former actions promised nothing but *matière pour rire*, did much cozen the world; for he came to the scaffold with good assurance and contempt of death. He was stayed by the sheriff, and told that there resteth yet something to be done, for that he was to be confronted with some other of the prisoners, but named none. So as Grey and Markham being brought back to the scaffold looked strange one upon the other, like men beheaded, and met again in the other world.

" Now all the actors being together on the stage, as one is at the end of the play, the sheriff made a short speech unto them by way of interrogatory of the heinousness of their offences, the justness of their trials, their lawful condemnation and due execution then to be performed, to all of which they assented. ' Then,' said the sheriff, ' see the mercy of your prince, who of himself hath sent hither a countermand and given you your lives.' There was no need to beg a plaudite of the audience, for it was given with such hues and cries that it went down from the castle into the town, and there began afresh, as if there had been some such-like accident.

" This resolution was taken by the King without man's help, and no man can rob him of the praise of yesterday's action, for the lords knew no other but that the execution was to go forward, till the very hour when it should be performed : and then calling them before him, he told them how much he had been troubled to resolve in this business ; for to execute Grey, who was a noble, young, spirited fellow, and save Cobham, who was as base and unworthy, were a manner of injustice. To save Grey, who was of a proud, insolent nature, and execute Cobham, who had shewed great tokens of humility and repentance, were as great a solecism ; and so went on with Plutarch's comparisons in the rest, still travelling in contrarities, but holding the conclusion in so indifferent balance that the lords knew not what to look for till the end came out—' and therefore I have saved them all.' "

Thus Raleigh remained in the Tower under sentence of death to be inflicted when the King should please, and the next stage of the story occurred some four years later. The prisoner had been living comfortably enough, enjoying the revenue of certain estates that had been spared him, and expecting to bequeath them to his son. But Robert Carr was now at court, penniless and dear to the King's heart. In an attempt to provide for him, James bethought him of Raleigh's land, in particular the manor of Sherborne, and put the lawyers on to find faults in the conveyance. It was easy to do and was done. In vain Raleigh fought the case ; in vain he sent his wife to plead. The King brushed her aside with a simple statement of necessity : " I maun ha' the land. I maun ha' it for Carr."

The last word, as is due, should lie with Raleigh, and if the first verses express his personal claim, the latter ones are his counter-charge to all the attacks of his enemies :

> Give me my scallop-shell of quiet,
> My staff of faith to walk upon ;
> My script of joy, immortal diet,
> My bottle of salvation,
> My gown of glory (hope's true gage)
> And thus I'll take my pilgrimage.
>
> Blood must be my body's balmer,
> No other balm will here be given,
> Whilst my soul, like quiet palmer,
> Travels to the land of heaven,
> Over all the silver Mountains,
> Where do spring those nectar fountains.
>
> And I there will sweetly kiss
> The happy bowl of peaceful bliss,
> Drinking mine eternal fill
> Flowing on each milky hill.
> My soul will be adry before,
> But after it will thirst no more.
>
> In that happy, blissful day,
>   More peaceful pilgrims I shall see,
>   That have cast off their rags of clay,
> And walk apparell'd fresh like me ;
>   I'll take them first,
>   To slake their thirst,
> And then taste of nectar suckets,
>   At those clear wells
>   Where sweetness dwells,
> Drawn up by saints in crystal buckets.

SIR WALTER RALEIGH

[face p. 100

And when our bottles and all we
Are fill'd with immortality,
Then those holy paths we'll travel,
Strew'd with rubies as with gravel ;
Ceilings of diamonds, sapphire floors,
High walls of coral and pearly bowers.
From thence to heaven's bribeless hall,
Where no corrupted voices brawl,
No conscience molten into gold,
No forg'd accuser bought and sold,
No cause deferr'd, no vainspent journey,
For there Christ is the King's attorney,
Who pleads for all without degrees,
And he hath angels, but no fees.
And when the grand twelve million jury
Of our sins, with direful fury,
'Gainst our souls black verdicts give,
Christ pleads his death, and then we live.
Be thou my speaker, taintless pleader,
Unblotted lawyer, true proceeder,
Thou givest salvation even for alms,
Not with a bribed lawyer's palms.
Then this is mine eternal plea,
To him that made heaven, earth and sea,
Seeing my flesh must die so soon
And want a head to dine next noon,
Just at the stroke of death, my arms being spread,
Set on my soul an everlasting head.
So shall I ready, like a palmer fit,
Tread those bless'd paths shown in Thy holy writ.

CHAPTER IX

CHURCH AND UNION

JAMES might be pleased enough to leave Scotland and enter on the richer pastures of England, but they were pastures with their full share of thistles. The quarrels of the Church were his first concern, and he must have entered into a consideration of them with a mind soured by the fierce disputes of Scotland. Presbyterianism in Scotland turned its eyes to Geneva and attempted to establish an unlovely tyranny which reduced the King, his counsellors, judges, and all the functions of civil life to unimportance beside the all-ruling Church. It was not merely that a deputation of ministers which waited on the King told him frankly that there were two kingdoms in Scotland and that in the kingdom of Jesus Christ, of which they were rulers, James VI was "not a king, not a lord, nor a head, but a member". It was that every minister thought himself competent to give his flock instructions about foreign policy, and these instructions were often in the highest degree treasonable and dangerous, and that the very jurisdiction of the King's courts in civil and criminal cases was usurped by synods of legally untrained men. When Brigham Young attempted to unify church and state, he was met by the hostility of the American continent. James's ministers were going farther and claiming to make the civil state the servant of the religious. These claims were as vast as that of the most assuming pope, and the religion that they offered was the bleakest and most repressive that human perversity ever invented. James had fought, not altogether unsuccessfully, to secure toleration for civil law and government, and he had come to England convinced of one thing, that a completely democratic organization of the Church, by giving the King no means of disciplining unruly members, was the surest way to promote trouble and possibly insurrection. He was not likely to listen to the enthusiastic Puritans with any particular friendliness.

On the other hand, something ought to be done. The English church was full of discontent and confusion, and no statesman could pretend that matters could be left alone. Bacon, looking round in his usual way for matters in which his advice might be helpful, drew up a little tract on the position of the church and the steps that he thought might be taken for its pacification. The whole thing is so characteristic of Bacon and throws so curious a light on the problems of the day that it is worth giving at least in a summary.

After the usual introduction proving partly by commonsense and partly by Latin tags that reform, so long as it be moderate and wise, is opposed to no law of God or man (perhaps an important point in those days), and further that in all indifferent things variety is not a vice, he goes on to take the chief difficulties and their possible remedies in turn.

The first point is the government of the church by bishops. This is good, but there are two points in their administration which have never satisfied him. The one is that they exercise their authority alone ;

the other that they are allowed to depute it. With
both of these points Bacon deals as a lawyer. Of all
the great offices of jurisdiction none is exercised by a
single man without assessors and counsellors. Yet
a bishop, whose powers are very large, sits alone,
and is only under an obligation to consult his dean
and chapter in financial matters. For the deputation
of their authority there is no sure ground either. All
over the world offices of confidence and skill cannot
be deputed; it is a breach of contract since the
appointment is made in the belief of personal sufficiency. A bishop is a judge of a high nature and
should leave his work to a deputy no more than a
judge of the High Court should.

As to the litany, God's house being a house of
prayer it is important, of the very essence of the
service. To extol it too much is to be superstitious,
to allow it to give place to extempore prayers is to
lose much of importance. It should be decent,
orderly, beautified by music and " quickened with
some shortness and diversity of prayers and hymns,
and with some interchanges of the voice of the people
as well as of the voice of the minister." There are
particular points that are not material but may be
settled according to commonsense or consideration
for others and in which the stronger may well give
way to the weaker. For example, the translation of
the Greek words as priest or minister; the baptism
of infants like to die by lay persons, as if baptism were
a vital necessity for the child's salvation; the arrangement of the service of confirmation, or the use of the
surplice in church.

Of all the reforms that were agitating the church,
the establishment of a preaching ministry was the

greatest. The great weapon of the Presbyterians and Puritans was the sermon, and the Church of England felt that its clergymen, many of whom could do little more than read the litany, were unable to compete with this organized power. Bacon's comments touch our sympathy. In an age when church-going was legally compulsory a preaching ministry, if it was not a very skilful one, might be anything but an advantage. It is good that the right man should preach, but " God forbid that every man that can take unto himself boldness to speak an hour together in a Church upon a text should be admitted for a preacher, though he mean never so well ". Preachers need training, and the Church should first train and then use them. Moreover, if the bishops took more care in choosing those whom they ordain, the standard of ministers would be higher, and lastly, if on a calculation it is found that there be not enough able ministers to serve all the parishes some pluralities should be allowed.

As for excommunication, a sentence which is given for the lightest causes and made a matter of fees, the method of inflicting it should be reformed, and it should only be inflicted by a bishop on due counsel. If any other penalty is required it should be some ordinary process in the ecclesiastical courts, which will reserve the high sentence of excommunication for occasions fitting its severity.

Non-residence and pluralities are a matter of need and the supply of ministers. As far as possible they should be prevented and where necessary small adjoining parishes amalgamated, or stipendiary preachers appointed to supply as they may places that are unfurnished.

The church is at present insufficiently supplied with funds. It is a law of religion that those who " feed the flock should live of the flock ", but it is not easy to see what is best to do. The Church was formerly too wealthy, but the land which was taken from it by Henry VIII cannot be restored. But of this point he does not think fit " to enter into further particularity or project ".

This paper, summing up the main points at issue, giving suggestions as to both law and expediency, was laid before the King on the eve of his conference with both parties at Hampton Court. On the first day James saw the bishops alone and all went well. The King showed off his powers of argument to a fairly complaisant audience and took up a position that was almost identical with Bacon's suggestions. On the next day he met Puritans, and was soon involved in a dispute with them. His temper at the meeting has often been made a charge of complaint against him, but with his experience of Scotland behind him and his habitual coarse speech, his final outburst is hardly to be wondered at. He told the Puritans that they were aiming at a " Scottish presbytery, which ", he said, " agreeth as well with a monarchy as God with the devil," and rammed his point home by an ingenious trope : " Stay, I pray you, for one seven years, before you demand that from me, and if then you find me pursy and fat, and my windpipes stuffed, I will perhaps harken to you ; for let that government be once up, I am sure I shall be kept in breath."

So victorious he left them, but what is really surprising is that when he came to draw up a list of reforms to be actually carried out he followed almost exactly the lines of Bacon's memorandum and added one which has left the most enduring glory on his reign of all his acts. He ordered the authorized translation of the Bible.

Concurrently with this conference Parliament met, and Bacon was undoubtedly the leading figure in the House of Commons. He serves on all committees, generally appearing first on the list. His advice receives more attention than that of other members, and had James possessed more prudence he would have recognized Bacon's position and made him the official leader of the House. Bacon had in fact no obvious rival. Not a single privy councillor had a seat in the lower House, the minor officials who sat there were very ordinary men, and when the government wanted to be specially represented Cecil had to come down and speak to the Commons, a task which he, not being a member of the House and not knowing their feelings, performed very imperfectly.

Fortunately for the King, Bacon was in no need of office to make him serve his interests, but he had no means of knowing the intricacies of government policy and he lacked the prestige which office would have given him. Bacon's history for the next few years is the history of James's relations with his parliaments.

The matter on which the King's heart was at the moment most set was the union of England and Scotland, and this proved no easy matter. In essence the difficulty arose from a well-founded English suspicion that the Scotch would commence a peaceful penetration of their land, and that the numerous and able offspring of Scotch manses would occupy all the more desirable positions south of the Tweed. But this deeper objection was at present cloaked under the

controversy over a name.   Suppose the lands were to
be united, *what was the resultant whole to be called?*
Bacon, speaking in the House, put forward what was
clearly the official view.   There were but two names
known of old for the island, Albion and Brittany, and
of these the one was poetical, so we must have the
other, and should follow in the steps of King Arthur
and Brutus.   As James himself made the comparison,
it is to be supposed that he enjoyed the idea of his
illustrious predecessors in title.   Further, he should
be King only, not Emperor, nor Great King, thus
showing his moderation when compared with Ger-
mans or Persians.   James clearly thought it a simple
matter.   Bacon, when he first spoke, seemed to see
no ground of opposition save conservatism.   But
conservatism was strong, and inside ten days Bacon
found himself, as reporter of the committee appointed
to consider the matter, called upon to set out a list
of objections, grouped under four heads, and calculated to show that the proposed use of a common name
would bring anarchy and chaos into the State at home
and the ruin of all treaties, honour and reputation
abroad.   For, as to the first head, there was no need
to change, and where there is no " urgent necessity
or evident utility " we should sit still ; and if we did
change, then the change of title would at the moment
of its execution abolish all laws, all oaths of allegiance,
all coronation oaths, in fact all legal acts in which
the King is spoken of as King of England.   The very
writs would fail to be efficacious, and the prisoner at
the bar might snap his fingers at the commissions of
those who tried him.

   Such a dreadful prospect at home was only equalled
by the confusion which would ensue abroad, when the

chancellories of Europe tore up as scraps of paper all the treaties which had been made with England.

Even the King was not exempt from this universal destruction. " The King's precedence before other Christian Kings, which is guided by antiquity of kingdoms and not by greatness, may be endangered, and his place turned last, because the newest."

Very last of all came the true reason, and Bacon, reading out this document to the house, must have smiled somewhat.

" The change of name will be harsh in popular opinion and unpleasing to the country."

The judges, when consulted, supported the Commons and declared the change impossible, so that the King gave way, not too graciously, and for a little while yet Englishmen avoided the name of Britons.

Meanwhile the serious business of the Union went on slowly. Committees sat and reported, conferred and reported again. Bacon's time was spent in taking notes and speaking from them, being compelled to represent, in conferences with the Lords, views which he did not hold, and trying to so rearrange James's rather tactless utterances that the House would let them pass without protest. Bacon's skill in all these activities was great. He was deep in the business. He could give advice officially, and was often listened to ; he seems to have commanded great confidence, to have offended no one ; and it is to be presumed that he enjoyed it all.

The King certainly approved, for in the summer vacation Bacon received his first reward for public service. He was forty-four years old and had been devoting himself to state business for over twenty years. He was now given a pension for life of £60, and had his appointment to the office of Learned Counsel, which he had held only by verbal warrant, granted to him by patent.

The other business of the vacation was preparation for the Great Commission on the Union of England and Scotland. Bacon began, in characteristic fashion, by writing to Sir Robert Cotton, the famous book-collector, and asking for his advice and an opportunity to talk the matter over. Then he composed a memorial to the King, setting out under headings the points of union and divergence that existed between the two countries, and what steps he thought might be taken about them. Further, to make things quite clear, he drew up a proclamation by which the King might assume the title of King of Great Britain and challenge the deluge that the Commons had threatened. Bacon's actual proclamation was not used, but the King, timing his actions well, published another on the same lines on October 20th, the very day on which the Commissioners for the Union were to meet. Thus the forty-eight Englishmen and thirty-one Scotch-men who were to arrange the terms of union started their deliberations when the Union was already accomplished—at least in the King's style and title—and the nation began its conjoint existence without any " contestation, difficulty or inconvenience ".

Of Great Commissions that have sat in England, this on the Union was probably the most expeditious and effective. It began its operations on October 29th and reported on December 6th, doing a piece of work of the first importance and one which has given steady satisfaction, in some six weeks. It is probable that Bacon was the most influential member of the committee, though he sat as a plain man among the dignitaries of England and Scotland. He had carefully prepared the ground. He, along with the Lord Advocate of Scotland, was entrusted with the task of drawing up the articles, and it is probable that it was his advice which determined the conventions of debate. The preface to the articles was entrusted to Cecil and Lord Fivye, but Bacon wrote one also, just in case it should be wanted, and in it he sets out the philosophic order behind the proceedings : " Forasmuch as we do find that hardly within the memory of all times there can be shewed forth a fit example or precedent of the work we have in hand, we thought ourselves so much the more bound to resort to the infallible and original ground of nature and common reason, and freeing ourselves from the leading or misleading of examples, to insist and fix our considerations upon the individual business in hand, without wandering or discourse."

Led on, then, by nature and common reason, they first repealed all hostile laws between the countries, secondly they made commerce free between the countries, thirdly they enabled real property to be held in either country, lastly they " provided that the justice of either realm should aid and assist, and not frustrate and interrupt, the justice of the other, especially in sundry cases criminal ".

All this was accomplished in great harmony and with only one dissentient voice.

But it took longer to deal with Parliament. Just after the commission reported, there was a scare of plague, then the Gunpowder Plot intervened, and it was only in 1606 that the Union was seriously discussed. Parliament was as hostile as it had been over the change of name, and the various parts of the act were only got through piecemeal. In the end, as with the name, the government took a back way, this time with the aid of the judges ; a test case was brought in Chancery, a Scotch infant was declared a natural subject of the King of England, and, without " contestation, difficulty or inconvenience ", the fundamental point of Union was achieved.

Chapter X

THE *ADVANCEMENT OF LEARNING*

In the brief interval of some nine months during 1605-1606, when Parliament was not sitting through fear of the plague, Bacon achieved two acts of note. He published his first important philosophical book, and he got married. He was now forty-five years old, advanced in years perhaps for either act, but the *Advancement of Learning* is the summary of a vast deal of reading and learning, and marriage was a matter which he entered upon only after due thought.

Bacon believed, and practised as he thought, that a man has no need to be a professional scholar to be learned, or that the life of a politician need not be so exacting that no time or thought remains for any higher functions. He was a man adept in fitting together the fragments of his life so that not a moment was lost and none of the complicated patterns was interrupted. It is a power not given to many. Anthony Trollope, though he was novelist and not philosopher, had it, and so have, to some extent, the growing number of people who on the continent are called the " working intelligentsia ". In Victorian days the author, the sage, the philosopher must be sheltered from the shocks of the world, the sordid cares, even the barking of his neighbour's dog. He was a being apart. But Bacon was modern. He could take his place in the affairs and business of the

day, and then go home and take up his studies where
he had left them overnight.   It is an art of attention,
it is also the power to hold firmly in the subconscious
one train of thought while exercising the conscious
mind on another.   The gift, if it be a gift and not
mere resolution and practice, is one of the most
convenient that a man can possess, and by its aid a
man can accomplish, as Bacon did, an amount of work
that seems phenomenal to persons who have not got
it.   When this power is accompanied by a quick
decision in business and a clear conception of what
work belongs to him and what to his neighbour,
efficiency is heightened.

It is objected " that learning should take up too
much time or leisure : I answer, the most active or
busy man that hath been or can be hath (no question)
many vacant times of leisure, while he expecteth the
tides and returns of business (except he be either
tedious and of no dispatch, or lightly and unworthily
ambitious to meddle in things that may be better done
by others) and then the question is but how those
spaces and times of leisure shall be filled and spent,
whether in pleasures or in studies."

Bacon spent his in studies, naturally and profitably.
He did not understand that the power to do so is not
given to everyone.   In such periods the materials for
the *Advancement of Learning* were collected and the
book written.

The first part is a defence of learning, and shows
both the discredits into which learning has fallen and
its true greatness.   It is an elaborate piece of writing
full of classical parallels and illustrations.   Here and
there is a keen observation or a pointed phrase, but
apart from the light which it throws on customs of the

day it has little interest. All we can learn from it is that scholars have long been open to the same charges, and that the joke about the oddities and shabbiness of the Heads of Oxford Colleges is as old as James I, and had about as much truth then as now.

" There is yet another fault which is often noted in learned men, that they do many times fail to observe decency and discretion in their behaviour and carriage, and commit errors in small and ordinary points of action, so as the vulgar sort of capacities do make a judgment of them in greater matters by that which they find wanting in them in smaller."

The second part of the book is more impressive. It is Bacon's proof that his youthful boast has been fulfilled. He had taken all knowledge for his province, and this is the description of the state in which he found that province to be. Taking the subjects of learning, he goes through them one by one, indicating what parts are deficient and where men might profitably apply their industry.

" History of nature is of three sorts : of nature in course, of nature erring or varying, and of nature altered and wrought—that is, history of creatures, history of marvels, and history of arts. The first of these no doubt is extant, and that in good perfection ; the two latter are handled so weakly and unprofitably, as I am moved to note them as deficient."

So dividing, arranging, judging.

The more interesting part of the book is its introduction, for there Bacon sets out his ideas on science, and in these he was the true prophet of modern development. It is hard to say what anyone ever learnt direct from Bacon. He was no scientist, he made no great discoveries, he lived and died an amateur, and yet his general ideas accord so exactly with the course that history has taken, that every laboratory might be decorated with his texts and every international society turn to him for a motto.

Bacon lived at a time when science, such as it was, belonged still to the Middle Ages, and knew much of " authority " and little or nothing of experiment. Nor did men work together or enjoy endowments. The most characteristic quality of modern science, after its experimental nature, is its co-operation. This is secured partly by the founding and endowing of great schools, partly by the publication of journals and international associations. All this Bacon foresaw as a necessity, and his mind was continually wondering how it could be achieved. At one time he had believed that if he became sufficiently great and rich he could himself start a band of workers. Then he realized that the task was too great for one man, and in any case preferment passed him by. He began to dream of a great college and call the task of founding it " kingly ". In his private notes he thinks the matter out concretely :

" Foundation of a college for Inventors. Two galleries with statues for Inventors past and spaces or bases for Inventors to come, and a library and an Inginary (? engine room). Allowance for travelling, Allowance for experiments ; Intelligence and corre-spondence with the Universities abroad.

" Question of the manner and praescripts touching secrecy, tradition and publication.

" Question of removes and expulsions in case within a time some invention worthy be not produced, and likewise question of the honors and rewards for inventions."

This college lived in Bacon's mind all his life, to appear in its grandest form in the *New Atlantis*. When he wrote for publication, he was more general but continued with the same ideas.

" First, therefore, amongst so many great foundations of colleges in Europe, I find strange that they are all dedicated to professions, and none left free to arts and sciences at large. . . . For if men judge that learning should be referred to action, they judge well, but they must not forget that it is these general studies which nourish all the professions and supply them with their powers." In fact, there must be a body of " disinterested " knowledge, acquired for its own sake, on which all subjects can draw. And so every true scientist thinks today.

" And because founders of colleges do plant and founders of lectures do water, it followeth well in order to speak of the defect which is in public lectures ; namely, in the smallness and meanness of the salary or reward which in most places is assigned unto them." A very modern complaint, and Bacon goes further even than modern reformers, and would pay the professor or lecturer a salary equal to that which he would receive if he practised his knowledge. For instance, one supposes the Professor of Law would draw the salary of a successful K.C. ! " Readers in sciences are indeed the guardians of the stores and provisions of sciences, whence men in active courses are furnished, and therefore ought to have equal entertainment with them.

" Another defect I note, wherein I shall need some alchemist to help me, who call upon men to sell their books and to build furnaces, quitting and forsaking Minerva and the Muses as barren virgins, and relying

upon Vulcan." Science is to become experimental,
and with heat and cold, depth and height wring from
nature her secrets. All this he foresaw would be
expensive—how expensive he probably did not
dream. " Therefore, as secretaries and spials of
princes and states bring in bills for intelligence, so
you must allow the spials and intelligencers of nature
to bring in their bills, or else you shall be ill advertised.

" Another defect which I note ascendeth a little
higher than the precedent. For as the proficience of
learning consisteth much in the orders and institutions
of universities in the same states and kingdoms, so
it would be yet more advanced if there were more
intelligence mutual between the universities of Europe
than there now is." Indeed there are international
organizations—such as the Jesuits. Why should not
learning copy the organization for a different end ?

This scheme for the reorganization of learning was
addressed to the King, as a monarch who possessed
intellectual abilities equal to its appreciation. It has
remained a prophecy, but one which did not begin to
be realized till near a century after its author was dead.

His second activity was crowned with more
immediate fruition.

Twice in his life Bacon is reported to have appeared
in all the bravery of purple velvet. He loved colours
and magnificence in dress, and he chose to celebrate
the two triumphs of his life in this manner. One was
his wedding day, the other when he rode in state to
take his seat in Chancery.

We first hear of Bacon's love in 1603, but only
indirectly. He is writing to Robert Cecil about other
matters and mentions the petition that he has made to

be knighted : " Lastly, for this divulged and almost prostituted title of knighthood, I could without charge, by your Honour's mean, be content to have it, both because of this late disgrace (he refers to financial troubles) and because I have three new knights in my mess at Gray's-Inn Commons, and because I have found out an alderman's daughter, an handsome maiden, to my liking. So if your Honour will find the time, I will come to the court from Gorhambury upon any warning."

The girl who had caught Bacon's eye belonged to a strange family, and one which a man of Bacon's prudence might have avoided. Alice Barnham, his sweetheart, was one of a family of seven. Her mother, Dorothy Barnham, the widow of an alderman, and with four daughters, had married John Packington and borne him three more children. Of this flock Alice was the eldest. Her mother, both in the ultimate number of her husbands and her treatment of them, is strongly reminiscent of the Wife of Bath. Alice's stepfather was a Worcestershire squire, a graduate of Oxford, a member of Lincoln's Inn, and a figure at court. He had amused Elizabeth by his strength and his joviality. He was a first-class swimmer, a man of sudden passions and wild extravagance. He ruined himself at court and petitioned for a gift. He was offered the land of a man condemned to lose his possessions ; but when he rode down and was met by a weeping wife and children, he turned tail and implored the Queen to restore the land. So he himself retired to his own estates of Hampton Lovet in Worcestershire, and there by economies saved enough to start building a great house at Westwood Park. Besides the house he made a great pond for swimming and to keep fish in. Unfortunately he made the water flow over part of an old road. It was easy enough to divert the track and he did it quite to his own satisfaction, but a neighbour, probably delighted at the opportunity of snubbing this high-handed squire, discovered the legal sanctity of roads, but promised not to press his rights so long as Packington behaved like a " good neighbour ". This Packington had no intention of doing. If he could not have his pond in his own way, by his own right, he would not have it at all. He cut his bund, the waters flowed in torrents over the countryside, fish lay gasping on the ploughed fields, and the Severn was discoloured for a week.

At a slightly later date he plunged into legal business and as Justice of the Peace for his shire resisted this regulation or enforced that with an excess of vigour and an absence of clear sense that makes him typical of many characters in fiction.

Bacon must have known him well at court, for he regularly passed part of the year in London living at a house in the Strand near the Savoy Church. Thither he brought his family, who were healthy country-bred children and doubtless inherited the vigour that both parents possessed so abundantly.

On May 10th, 1606, Bacon was married at the Chapel of S. Marylebone. A pretty country wedding, and it is to be hoped that the sun shone as they rode out between the green hedgerows. The bride was young, under twenty, perhaps only fifteen, and according to the custom of the time would be married with her hair loose about her and her dress covered with ribbons and lover's knots. After the ceremony all the young men of the party would snatch at the knots and at the bride's ribbon garters and carry them off to wear as favours.

Of another wedding it was written : " She was led to church between two sweet boys, with bride-laces and rosemary tied about their silken sleeves. Then was there a fair bride-cup of silver and gilt carried before her, wherein was a goodly branch of rosemary, gilded very fair, hung about with silken ribands of all colours : next was there a noise of musicians that played all the way before her . . ."

Francis and Alice would have all the pageantry of the time, for the bridegroom loved it ; and the wedding ring, which was jewelled then, before the Puritans turned it to plain gold, was doubtless as bright and shining as he could procure. For their subsequent adornment Bacon made such preparations that the gossips of the day noted it.

" Sir Francis Bacon was married yesterday to his young wench in Maribone Chapel. He was clad from top to toe in purple, and hath made himself and his wife such store of fine raiments of cloth of silver and gold that it draws deep into her portion. The dinner was kept at his father-in-law's, Sir John Packington's lodging over against the Savoy, where the chief guests were the three knights, Cope, Hicks and Beeston (three of Cecil's secretaries), and upon this conceit (as he said himself) that since he could not have my Lord of Salisbury (Cecil) in person, which he wished, he would at least have his representative body."

The match was by the standards of the time a very suitable one. We should think the disparity in age over-great, for Bacon was forty-six, but that was in accordance with custom. Every other woman in

Elizabethan days seems to be a widow, or to be enjoying her second or third husband. That is natural. A woman's expectation of life is as good or better than a man's. She was less likely to perish untimely on the scaffold, and starting her married life twenty years before her mate she could easily survive him, and yet not be past her prime. No one therefore would have felt that Alice was taking a husband too old for her.

On the financial side the match was also fitting. Alice brought landed property valued at about £120 a year and had expectations of inheriting a thousand or so after her mother's death. Bacon was able to settle on her £500 a year, and he seems by this time definitely to be started on the path of financial prosperity.

With his wife he seems to have lived in peace and quietness. There was no scandal, and Bacon has been condemned as a subject for a biography because " he has no private life ".

Bacon had no children, and it is hard to imagine him as a very ardent husband. What he does express in letters to friends is a very temperate satisfaction. He seems to have been contented with his marriage, and till the year of his death we hear no word of friction, disloyalty or unkindness. Bacon in the few completely natural letters we possess wrote charmingly; he probably talked in the same way, and the tone of merry courtesy was doubtless for his wife as well as his men friends. But he was not an open man of sentiment, nor did men in the seventeenth century expect quite the same companionship from their wives as we do today. A letter which deals with a piece of business but which illustrates both Bacon's friendly tone and the way in which he could allude to his marriage is worth quoting. Bacon is writing after the death of a friend to one with whom he has business as an executor. "Good Cousin, no man knoweth better than yourself what part I bear in grief for Mr. Bettenham's departure. For in good faith I never thought of myself at better liberty than when he and I were by ourselves together . . .

"Your loving congratulations for my doubled life, as you call it, I thank you for. No man may better conceive the joys of a good wife than you yourself, with whom I dare not compare. But I thank God I have not taken a thorn out of my foot to put it into my side. For as my state is somewhat amended, so I have no other circumstance of complaint. But herein we will dilate when we meet, which meeting will be much more joyful if my Lady hear a part in the music, to whom I pray let me be commended."

More curious is his essay on marriage, published just a year after his wedding. He has not a word about the ecstasy of love, and, unlike his essay on friendship, which experience of life caused him to rewrite entirely, the few lines which he added to the essay later contain no new thoughts.

"He that hath wife, and children, hath given hostages to fortune; for they are impediments to great enterprises, either of virtue or of mischief.

"Certainly wife and children are a kind of discipline of humanity and single men are more cruel and hard-hearted, good to make severe Inquisitors.

"Grave natures led by custom and therefore constant are commonly loving husbands. Chaste women are often proud, and froward as presuming upon the merit of their chastity. It is one of the best bandes both of chastity and obedience in the wife if she think her husband wise, which she will never do if she find him jealous. Wives are young men's mistresses, companions to men of middle age, and old men's nurses. So as a man may have a quarrel to marry when he will, but yet he was reputed one of the Wise Men that made answer to the question *when a man should marry*, a younger man not yet, an elder man not at all."

But if he lived quietly with his wife, he had troubles with his relations. Lady Packington, having quarrelled violently with her husband, turned her sharp tongue and fierce temper on her sons-in-law. Bacon was trustee for the younger daughter's settlement, and it fell to him to write the letter telling his mother-in-law that he meant her children to live at peace even if she could not manage to do so herself. The letter is so sharp in tone, so much the writing of a confident man, that it apparently awed even Lady Packington into quiescence.

MADAM,

You shall with right good will be made acquainted with anything which concerneth your daughters, if you bear a mind of love and concord. Otherwise you must be content to be a stranger unto us. For I may not be so unwise as to suffer you to be an author or occasion of dissension between your daughters and their husbands, having seen so much misery of that kind in yourself.

And above all things I will turn back your kindness, in which you say you will receive my wife if she be cast off. For it is much more likely we have occasion to receive you being cast off, if you remember what is passed. But it is time to make an end of these follies. And you shall at this time pardon me this one fault of writing to you. For I mean to do it no more till you use me with respect as you ought. So wishing you better than it seemeth you will draw upon yourself, I rest

Yours,

CHAPTER XI

PRIVATE MEDITATIONS

In 1607, when Bacon was forty-seven, he received at last his first step of official promotion. He became Solicitor-General, quietly, without canvass or opposition. The private affairs with which his mind was occupied at the time are known to us better than at any other occasion. Bacon had a habit of writing down anything that seemed important or that he wanted to remember in a notebook. One of these books, of the year 1608, has been preserved and can be seen in the British Museum. From it we have a section of his thoughts, arranged roughly into groups, and can tell what matters he turned over with himself when he had leisure to order his mind. What makes them more interesting is that they were private notes for his own eyes only, and that Bacon was before all things honest. He had the power to know what he was doing and the precision of expression which recorded it exactly. The average man has generally only the haziest notion of his purposes and that notion escapes his fumbling words. It thus seems that Bacon is cynical or base in some of his thoughts. There is in some men's minds all the difference between doing a thing and meditating clearly on the doing. The lawyers have seized on the difference, and in pre-psychological ages decided that if there is no evidence of premeditation the act is less guilty than if there were ; being due, they suppose, in the former

case to the blind chances of the moment. They forget
that impulses may lie just below the clear level of
thought, out of the reach of most men's words, but
yet be there and be nourished all the same. Bacon's
mind was a lucid one and his words were equal to the
task of revealing his impulses.

A fair example of this verbal lucidity is his scheme
of notebooks—all written out fair, while another
man would have simply acted. He had been accustomed to keeping three sets of notebooks, each set
divided into a journal of things or thoughts which
occurred from day to day, and a " kalender of titles
of things of the same nature, for better help of
memory and judgment ". These three sets of books
received (1) " all remembrances private of what
nature soever," (2) " all particulars but yet such as I
think worthy to enter at large," and (3) account books.
He now proposes in all solemnity to make a change.

" I think it will be more ready and more easy to
make these divisions of paper books fewer and less
curious and more sorted to use than art ; and therefore
first to have *comentarius solutus* like a merchant's wast
book where to enter all manner of remembrance of
matter, fortune, business, study, touching myself,
service, others, either sparsim or in schedules, without
any manner of restraint, only then to be divided into
two books, the one *transportata ex comentario vetere*,
containing all manner notes already taken in several
paper books fitt to be retained, the other *comentarius
novus*. Then to have another book like to the merchant's legger book wherein those things which
deserve it are sett down in the comentary briefly at the
first leisure. . . . And thirdly out of that book to
make several title books wherein things of a nature

may be (by the labour of a servant in part) entered in order and under fit titles."

Of this hierarchy of remembrances, our book is of the lowest grade, the first fruits of the new order, being the first division consisting of notes from previous books and judged still valuable.

As recorded in this book, his first and last thoughts are for his legal business and advancement. Mixed together are notes of cases about which he must advise or be ready for next term, thoughts how he may offer his services to the King, notes on his bearings to particular persons. The dominating spirit of the day was Cecil, now Lord Salisbury, and to him Bacon's thoughts continually return. No one who has watched the incessant self-advertisement and morigeration (to use Bacon's word) which goes on among a group of modern civil servants, who have little to hope and less to fear, can wonder if Bacon, with his feet upon the slippery footpath of court favour, had to look to pleasing those in power. Before his eyes already danced the Chancellorship, and his optimistic nature led him to hope that Cecil might be won sufficiently to let him attain it.

The cases which he had to consider numbered about twenty-eight, and among them were such pieces of personal service as preparing a memorandum against the next meeting of Parliament, and carrying on the task of equalizing the laws of England and Scotland. There were suits for patents that had to be looked into. Mr. Sutton had a project for founding a great charitable institution, which became the Charterhouse, and Bacon was lobying the Archbishop of Canterbury in the matter. There were the laws concerning recusants, a fierce dispute about the jurisdiction of the councils of the Marches and the North, and Bacon reminds himself that he must peruse " the kalenders against next term yet better, calling for those that want and thinking of other courses for increase of practice ".

All this shows a man determined to succeed in his profession by hard work and attention to business, but these characteristics were not enough then to assure success—any more than they are today in the position in which Bacon was. Personal influence reigned supreme and gossip was more powerful than anything but gold. Bacon had quite definite views on the use of influence and the extent to which one man might honourably try to influence another. In the *Advancement of Learning* he sets them out as an answer to one of the charges made against scholars.

" Another fault incident commonly to learned men is that they fail sometimes in applying themselves to particular persons. . . . This is no inability, but a rejection upon choice and judgment. For the honest and just bounds of observation of one person by another extend no further but to understand him sufficiently, whereby not to give him offence, or whereby to be able to give him faithful counsel, or whereby to stand upon reasonable guard and caution in respect of a man's self. But to be speculative unto another man to the end to know how to work him, or wind him, or govern him, proceedeth from a heart that is double and cloven and not entire and ingenuous, which as in friendship it is want of integrity, so towards princes or superiors is want of duty."

Holding these views, and acting on them, Bacon's suggestions for his own aggrandisement are rather pathetic than otherwise.

" To correspond with Salisbury in a habite of natural but no ways perilous boldness, and in vivacity, invention, care to cast and enterprise, but with due caution," or " To furnish my Lord of Salisbury with ornaments for public speeches. To make him think how he should be reverenced by a Lord Chancellor—if I were he."

And in more general wise. " To have particular occasions, fitt and grateful and contynual, to maintain private speach with every great person and sometimes drawing more than one of them together. This especially in public places and without care or affectation."

To have to note all this down betrays that Bacon was no courtier born. Indeed, as a man of intrigue, he was sadly deficient. One interesting fact is that he was never even offered a Spanish pension. Cecil, James's chief minister, held one, and as it was not only maintained but increased it is to be supposed that he gave value for his money. Numerous other men of no more influence and far less ability than Bacon received their £1,000 a year, but Bacon never even had the offer. And yet, at the end of his life, Gondomar, the Spanish Ambassador, was a more faithful friend to him than any of his own countrymen. It was not that he hated Spain; his honesty and his lack of suppleness in court intrigue made him too respected to be a pensioner.

Besides his meditations on his own official life, he had thoughts on general policy. In the notes they are so abbreviated as to be obscure, but it seems that he was wondering how best to improve the King's position and had hit on the scheme of making England the head of an empire in the West. The notes run :

9

" Persuade the King in glory ' Aurea condet saecula.'
The fairest, without disorder or peril, is the general
persuading to King and People, and course of infusing
everywhere the foundation in this isle of a monarchy
in the West, as an apt seat, state, people for it : so
civilizing Ireland, further colonizing the wild of
Scotland, annexing the Low Countries."

These projects were very real in Bacon's mind and
even determined his action, for he continually strove
to improve conditions in Ireland and even looked
farther afield. He was one of the commission which
looked after the planting of the colony in Virginia
and which saved the colonists from destruction by a
short-sighted " company ".

Besides these public matters, there were his domestic
affairs. In especial money. Bacon was now comparatively rich. He had a town house, apart from his
Gray's Inn chambers, for his wife, and his country
house at Gorhambury. He had various farms producing a rent roll of about £330 a year. His offices
and practice produced :

	£
My pension	60
My solicitor's place	1,000
My practice	1,200
My office of Starchamber	2,000
My Duchy fee	20

In addition there was his wife's fortune of about £220
a year and sundry other small sums, so that his total
annual income was about £5,000. In addition he had
personal estate of furniture and jewels to the extent
of about £2,000. The curious thing is that Bacon
was still in debt to the extent of some £4,500 and

rather more than half of this was bearing interest, probably at ten per cent. He speculates on means to improve his estate, reminds himself of some leases that he must renew, wonders if he shall have some woodlands surveyed in the hope of making more out of them, and writes down certain debts owing to him as desperate.

Bacon's efforts to improve his husbandry were as unsuccessful, though less obviously so, as his projects to get on good terms with Cecil. In his essay on *Expense* he had some very proper remarks about the relation between a man's income and his expenditure.

" Certainly, if a man will keep but of even hand, his ordinary expenses ought to be but to the half of his receipts, and if he think to wax rich, but to the third part."

But in his own life he was prodigal and careless to a degree. He regularly spent the whole of his income, and was always in debt. It is said that his servants would help themselves to handfuls of coins from the drawer where the cash was kept, and no one held themselves responsible. It is certain that Bacon never, from the time when he disputed Mr. Trott's debt but had to rely on his memory for the sums that had passed on either side, to the end of his life kept proper accounts ; although there are indications that now and then, as in the present case, he made attempts to do so. In all his huge household there might have been one man who could be trusted to do it.

Three other matters occupy his mind : his literary projects, his home, and his health. In the mood of the *Advancement of Learning* Bacon is casting about for persons to interest in his project, for schemes of ideal colleges, or, failing that, the "laying for a place to command witts and pens, Westminster, Eton, Winchester, especially Trinity College in Cambridge, St. John's in Cambridge, Magdalen College in Oxford, and bespeaking thus betimes with the King, my Lord Archbishop and my Lord Treasurer." He had a scheme, such as frequently enters the heads of modern colleges, for playing the *captator* and acquiring a legacy with which to start his scientific foundation.

"Not desisting to draw in the Bp. Aund, being single, rich, sickly, a professor to some experiments."

Even the prisoners in the Tower, who presumably had abundant leisure, might be made use of.

"The setting to work my Lord of Northumberland and Raleigh, themselves being already inclined to experiments."

He then draws up a table of the enquiries which might be undertaken, which are fifteen, and in particular he draws out his investigation into motion with great elaboration.

He next turns to a matter more within his own hands, the improvement of the pond-yard at Gorhambury. From this time on he is always improving his house and gardens there till they became noted and a byword.

> That spatious, specious, precious refectorie,
> Which cost a world of wealth (so saith the story)
> Those pebble paved brooks, empaled lakes,
> Thick clad with countless sholes of ducks and drakes.

He spared neither money nor trouble, and he indulged all his tastes for elaborate ornament and bright colours and scents. His water garden was to be enclosed with a brick wall and fruit trees planted upon it.

Without were to be trees, birches on two sides, limes on the other two, some ten feet distant from the wall, so that the wall might hide most of the trunks and only the branches appear above. Within was to be a raised walk twenty-five feet broad. This walk would resemble the raised walks at Hampton Court or Penshurst and it would slope down to a stream. The banks were to be turfed and mown and no trees were to be there, only a few fine standard roses. The stream was to flow along over a bed of gravel and fine pebbles and to murmur and tinkle, besides being clear to the eye. Within this stream was to be another walk, also twenty-five feet wide and bordered with all sorts of irises and lilies. Within this walk was to be the actual lake, and it was to be fenced, and on the rail gilt images and coloured glass placed to catch the sun and glitter. Along the edges where the bigger flowers did not grow were to be violets and strawberries for scent. In the lake was to be one big island with a " house for freshness with an upper gallery open upon the water, a terrace above that, and a supping room open under that ; a dining room, a bedchamber, a cabanett and a room for music, a garden ". Besides the big island, to which a bridge led, there were to be little islands with statues, on one a hornbeam with a seat, on another a rock, on a third a grotto, and there was to be a little boat to go about between them.

Bacon, having devised this charming place for idling, goes on to his personal health. Like most men of his day, he suffered from constipation, due partly to habitual over-eating, partly to a lack of the simpler remedies we use today. A bottle of medicinal paraffin would have rendered life very different and saved countless hours of discomfort. Bacon suffered not only physically but mentally, and now and then was afflicted by " melancholy, with strangeness in beholding and darkness ". He notes : " When I was last at Gorhambury, I was taken much with my symptom of melancholy and doubt of present peril. I found it first by occasion of soppe with sack taken middle meal and it continued with me that night and the next morning, but note that it cleared and went from me without purge and I turned light and disposed of my self." These ailments, which perhaps would in a lesser man be dismissed as " fits of the blues ", were due at least in part to causes other than physical ones. " I have found now twice upon amendment of my fortune disposition to melancholy and distaste, especially the same happening against the long vacation when company failed and business both ; for upon my solicitor's place I grew indisposed and inclined to superstition." The compilation of this notebook, being a work of such a time, and containing records of symptoms, was perhaps an attempt to combat his ailment by providing himself with business.

For his more ordinary ailments he relied on remedies which are still in use today. He took milk of almonds or some other mild acid, such as lemon juice, at meals, and he used massage " sub hypochondriis and the region of my belly under the navel ". This to increase his appetite and produce more regular action. He made himself an iron tonic, steeping iron in wine and drinking the liquid. At one time he tried a diet of " boiled meat, cool salads, abstinence of wine ", and though it did him much good, he discontinued it for " palling and weakening his stomach ".

He was at his worst in the afternoon and fell back on the modern method of getting over that trying hour.

" I do find nothing to induce stopping more and to fill the head and to induce languishing and distaste and feverish disposition more, I say, than any manner of offer to sleep at afternoon, either immediately after dinner or at four o'clock. And I could never yet find resolution and strength enough in myself to inhibit it. I have ever had opinion that some comforting drink at four o'clock hour, which is the hour of my languishing, were proper for me."

Alas for Bacon, tea was not yet in England !

This notebook exhibits Bacon as a man of the most complex business. As Solicitor, he had the work of his office, as a parliamentarian, the work of that. He claimed to advise the King on all matters of importance, and his head was full of schemes for the public good. He had the management of a large property, and the anxieties of one seeking court favour. He was planning one of the great works of science and philosophy, and actively engaged in producing a complete description of nature. He had the beautifying of a country house on his mind, and, instead of turning his health over to the family doctor and doing what he was told, he was playing physician to himself and actively experimenting on the cure of an awkward distemper. There can have been very few men in the history of the world with a capacity for business and a clearness of mind that would enable them to deal with so much at once. In the rare cases when lawyers and politicians are also philosophers, they do not generally sit as Members of Parliament or take up experimental science—in however rudimentary a state it may be.   Bacon, so far as we know, neglected nothing.   He even found time to evolve or collect epigrams which he thought would come in some day :

" Death comes to young men and old men go to death.   That is all the difference."

It is not to be wondered at that he needed a series of notebooks.

CHAPTER XII

KING AND PARLIAMENT

JAMES was perpetually short of money, and his pecuniary embarrassments were those of the Chancellor of the Exchequer and a spendthrift gentleman. Today these embarrassments are separated and the King is the chief recipient on the civil list and suffers domestically what he may, while the Chancellor of the Exchequer shoulders the financial burdens of the country as a whole. Parliament assumes ultimate responsibility both for providing the King with maintenance, and for conducting the administration and defence of the country. In Stuart days the position was completely reversed. It was the King who must support the country. From his own resources, the produce of his lands, his feudal dues, his customs and so forth he must supply himself, his court, army, navy, officials and judges. Parliament was called on to help, but if it refused, if it said " This is no affair of ours ", the King must manage as best he could, and forego a service of plate to pay a judge or pledge his royal credit for the means to entertain an ambassador.

Queen Elizabeth was a mistress of economy. She was also on good terms with the nation, and what she asked from Parliament was granted. James was very differently situated. By nature he was prodigal, and his hosts of followers saw to it that his natural proclivities received every encouragement. Elizabeth

had been wont to reward her favourites by the grant
of a monopoly; public opinion took away from
James that inexpensive form of remuneration. Moreover, James was not in sympathy with his subjects;
he waged no popular wars, he touched no imaginations, no poets hymned him as they had sung Gloriana
and the Virgin Queen—a garrulous, self-opinionated
Scotchman was no theme for poets even had there
been poets to sing.

> The silver swan that living had no note
> When death approached unlocked her silent throat,
> Leaning her breast against the reedy shore,
> Thus sang her first and last—then sang no more :—
> Farewell all joys.   O Death, come close my eyes
> More geese than swans now live, more fools than wise.

And James lost the financial benefits of the moment,
as well as the posthumous glories which might have
accrued to him had he been able to inspire his subjects
to sing.

Further, when money did fall into his hands, he
used it in such a way that he alienated the sympathy
even of those who might naturally have approved.
Laws were in force fining those who refused to
attend church. Feeling in general was always in
favour of enforcing the penalties against the recusants,
but when gentlemen were deprived of their land and
the money bestowed on two footmen, no body of
English opinion could fail to receive a wound. In
1607 things were even worse, for James authorized a
kind of blackmail, of which his Scottish courtiers
reaped the chief harvest. Many whose lands could
have been legally confiscated were allowed to retain
them at the price of bribing certain courtiers, to
whom they were assigned. If these bribes did not

come up to expectation, the land was finally seized and passed into the hands of the tormentors.   Thus a system closely resembling that of the *delators* of the Roman Empire was instituted, and an English House of Commons, who had passed an act to benefit their own church, saw it being exploited for the enrichment of those very needy Scots whom they had tried so hard to keep out of their country.   They must have been confirmed in their view that the Union of the countries was a mistake.   Naturally, therefore, Parliament viewed James's demands for money with doubt.

He had begun badly.   Elizabeth had left the Treasury exhausted, and the Irish wars were a continual drain on his finances.   At the beginning of his reign it was noted :

" Out of Ireland here are come many captains with their pockets full of brass, and sue to have it made good silver ; but the Lord Treasurer's skill is not that of alchymy.   The coffers are so empty that household officers are unpaid, and the pensioners and guard are ready to mutiny."

Nor did things become any easier.   In 1606, when they were still excited over the Gunpowder Plot, the Commons had passed an unprecedentedly large grant of three subsidies, i.e. about £403,413.   But four years were allowed for its collection, and it was accompanied by a petition of grievances which caused the King no small annoyance.   On other occasions they were less liberal, and James was hopelessly in debt.   His ordinary expenditure exceeded his ordinary revenue by £83,000 a year and there was a debt of over a million.   Parliament was definitely unfriendly, so that when, in 1608, on the death of the old Treasurer,

Robert Cecil took over the post, and added it to the
Secretaryship which he already held, one hardly
knows whether to consider him a hero or braggart.
His financial administration was conspicuously unlucky and his management of Parliament clumsy in
the extreme.

His first expedient was perhaps suggested by his
experiences over the Union of England and Scotland.
If Parliament will not do what it should, circumvent
it.   The King possessed the right to impose customs
duties.   A squabble of the moment reminded his
ministers vividly of the matter and Cecil apparently
thought that here was the weapon to his hand.   So
only twenty-two days after taking office, he set out
and, " attended by the Chancellor and Barons of the
Exchequer, went to the Custom House, and there in
the Assembly of the Chief Merchants of England,
assembled from all the principal parts of the land, did
make an excellent speech to prove that Impositions
might lawfully be imposed by sovereign kings and
princes on all merchandise issuing out and coming
into their ports ".   His speech was apparently so
persuasive " that every man, after some little contradiction " consented to the laying of a general
customs duty, which excluded only the poor man's
bread and beer.   The sanguine subordinate who drew
up the account felt sure that it would " prove the most
gainful to the King and his posterity of any one day's
work done by any one Lord Treasurer since the time
of King Edward III ".   Instead it was to be a hornet's
nest, for Parliament, seeing quite clearly the pos-
sibilities of this method of raising revenue, put it into
the forefront of their grievances and were prepared to
contest it to the death.

But though the same subordinate reckoned that Cecil had in two and a half months gotten the King " in money £37,455 and in yearly revenue £71,100 ", this was not nearly enough to keep things square, and if he was to prevent a disaster Cecil must appeal to Parliament.   And here he embarked on a course which, while it expressed the facts of the situation, was so unwise as to be the root of infinite future trouble. At the moment the King and Commons were at cross-purposes, and for this very reason, that the King did nothing but ask them for money, and refused to allow them to deal with grievances, except by way of petition, and gave them no encouragement to think about general affairs of state.   Now Bacon had a theory which he held all his life, that no Parliament ought to be called on money questions only.   Parliament should be called to discuss the state of the country, and should have suggested to it some topic on which it could profitably legislate.   Bacon, writing a little later to the King, explains the point fully : " My third proposition is that this Parliament may be a little reduced to the more ancient form which was to voice the Parliament to be for some other business of estate and not merely for money ; but that to come in upon the bye, whatsoever the truth be. I mean it not in point of dissimulation but in point of majesty and honour ; that the people may have somewhat else to talk of and not wholly of the King's estate, and that Parliament-men may not be wholly possessed of these thoughts.   What shall be the causes of estate given forth ad populam, whether the opening and increase of trade, or whether the plantation of Ireland, or the reduction and recompiling of laws, it may be left to further consideration.   But I am settled in this, that somewhat be published beside the money matter, and that in this form there is much advantage."

A Parliament thus summoned had, as Bacon pointed out, something to think about, some useful work to do, would feel itself of consequence in the state, and therefore be more ready to assist in financing the state. A Parliament summoned merely to provide money, over whose spending it would have practically no control, felt neither dignified nor an equal partner, and therefore was only too ready to show its power by a refusal.

Cecil, however, did not think so. He had no respect for the House of Commons, and did not pretend any. He summoned them up to a conference with the Lords and proceeded to make a speech in which he set out quite plainly and baldly the national balance sheet and suggested that they should supply the deficiencies. A reasonable enough proceeding if Parliament had loved the King, or if they had had any control of the spending of the money they voted. As things were, he felt bound to suggest a return for the money required, and hinted vaguely that if they would pay up the King would on his side provide " a general redress of all just grievances ".

The House of Commons were thus being invited to take part in a bargain as between hostile contracting parties. Or, if they were not hostile, at least their interests were as different as those of a merchant and purchaser, who chaffer over the price of a commodity. Events had, in truth, brought the King and his Parliament to this pass, but to admit it publicly, to make it the basis of policy was an error of first-class importance. In some cases if things are bad it is better to admit it, but in human relationships skilful hypocrisy, coupled with remedial measures, will do far more than a blank statement of truth. The King and Parliament should be partners in the government of the realm. Pretend that they are and they probably will develop into it ; declare that they are opposed to each other and a revolution is the natural outcome.

Bacon believed in both King and Parliament, but of the two he believed most in the monarchy. In consequence, when once Cecil had proposed his Great Contract, he did his best to further it and to secure to the King an adequate income. The Commons, however, were full of suspicion. In the first place, having no neutral third party to hold the stakes, and each believing that the other would welsh, the Commons would not grant the money till their grievances were redressed, and the court would do nothing about grievances till it had the money. Further, Cecil's attitude had revealed to the Commons their power. The King was on the verge of bankruptcy. They could keep him there till they got their own way. Were they likely to pay his debts, give him a permanent income larger than he had ever enjoyed before, and so set him free to do as he liked ? Not they. Thus when, through weary negotiations, undignified bargaining, the parties had approached a settlement, a few months' holiday in their constituencies and thinking it over changed the mind of the Commons. They returned convinced that, as the King's poverty seemed to inflict no inconvenience on anybody but himself and those court officials and favourites whom they disliked, they would leave him to suffer, and try to get their grievances redressed without parting with the power which would enable them to do so.

For two years the discussions lasted, and in this time the King's credit was destroyed. The country grew accustomed to the thought and even the use of their new position and power, and in the end the King was forced to dissolve Parliament without having received any assistance, and having had to submit, as he felt, to " more disgraces, censures and ignominies than ever Prince did endure ".

This was Cecil's last great business, for next year he died. What men thought of him may be judged from two sources. Bacon, writing to the King immediately after his death, says: " He was a fit man to keep things from growing worse, but no very fit man to reduce things to be much better." When some months had passed, he could speak a little more freely. Commenting on the hopes of a peaceful Parliament, he says: " The Earl of Salisbury has taken a great deal of envy and carried it away in a chariot into the other world." Considering that Bacon had been thwarted by Cecil all his life, had been his cousin and yet never written him a familiar letter, and frankly breathed more freely when he was gone, it is a moderate and slightly humorous statement. Others spoke differently and an epitaph, attributed to Raleigh, went the round of court. James laughed and said that he hoped the writer would die before he did.

> Here lies Hobinall our pastor while ere,
> That once in a quarter our fleeces did shear ;
> To please us, his cur he kept under clog,
> And was ever after both shepherd and dog.
> For oblation to Pan his custom was thus,
> He first gave a trifle, then offered up us :

SERO SED SERIO

ROBERT CECIL, EARL OF SALISBURY

And through his false worship such power he did gain,
As kept him o' th' mountain, and us on the plain.
Where many a hornpipe he tun'd to his Phyllis,
And sweetly sang Walsingham to's Amaryllis,
Till Atropos clapt him (a pox on the drab),
For (spite of his tar box) he died of the scab.

We still do not love Chancellors of the Exchequer, but we spare comments on their private lives.

Chapter XIII

ATTORNEY GENERAL

On Cecil's death Bacon undoubtedly heaved a sigh of relief. He had felt during his cousin's long tenure of power as " a hawk tied to another's fist, that mought sometimes bait and proffer but could never fly ". And now Cecil was gone, leaving vacant two of the greatest posts in the Government, the Secretaryship and the Treasurership, and having trained up no one to succeed him. Bacon, surveying the position and considering frankly what work he could do of utility, thought that he might become Secretary and leader of the House of Commons. With this in his mind, he wrote to the King, making a tentative offer of his services, but the King did not accept him. Instead James procrastinated, delayed the appointment of a Secretary, decided not to summon Parliament and put the Treasury into commission.

So Bacon once more settled down to his legal work, to his parliamentary duties, to efforts to improve the King's revenue without appealing to Parliament, and to literature. The great cases of the day passed through his hands ; he drew up elaborate memorials on the matter of the King's estates, lengthy schedules of economies effected or about to be effected ; he boasted, as spokesman of the commissioners that he had improved His Majesty's revenue by £35,776 a year, and got in some £309,680 by extraordinary collections. But unfortunately even so the budget did not balance ;

for the annual deficit was by now £160,000 and the debt half a million. So, as befalls other commissions engaged in curing something rotten in the state of England, the conscientious labours of the members may have applied the brake, but still left the country heading straight for destruction.

By far the most important event to Bacon was his promotion in 1613 to be Attorney General. This he achieved by an ingenious rearrangement of posts, and it is interesting to notice that Bacon is now sufficiently in authority to dispose of other men's lives as well as his own. In this case it was Coke who became a pawn in his game.

For some years past now Coke had been Chief Justice of the Common Pleas, and had been engaged in establishing the rights of the Common Law of England. One of the first fields attacked had been the provincial jurisdictions which drew their authority from the general jurisdiction of the old Council. Not only had the King's Council been the supreme legal body in the realm, but it had had power to delegate its functions, and had set up councils in the North and in the Marches of Wales where, for convenience, less important cases, especially civil ones, could be settled. This jurisdiction had not been too well administered, and Worcestershire, finding itself aggrieved under the jurisdiction of the Council of the Marches, and having Sir John Packington as its violent champion, had appealed to Westminster and been supported by Coke. The zeal with which Coke took up the cause of the shire, or indeed any other malcontents, had probably two sources. He really believed in the importance of the independence of the Common Law, and judges in his day were as anxious

as any other practitioners to increase the volume of
business that passed through their courts. The
reason was simply that a very small part of their
incomes was made up of direct salary, all the rest came
from court fees. As a result judges vied with each
other in inventing legal fictions that would expedite
business, and English law progressed by the blessed
force of competition. If Coke could free Worcestershire and its neighbours from the jurisdiction of
the Council, all those cases would flow into Westminster and the metropolitan judges would benefit
accordingly.

As Chief Justice of the Common Pleas, Coke had
every opportunity of annoying the Government.
What Bacon suggested in 1613 was that Coke might
receive the higher but less lucrative post of Chief
Justice of the King's Bench; Hobart might become
Chief Justice of the Common Pleas; he himself might
take the Attorneyship thus vacated, and Yelverton
could become Solicitor. By this shuffle he would
get the office he wanted, and Coke would receive a
kind of discipline, by the decrease in emoluments,
though without disgrace; and moreover in his new
post he would have less opportunity of quarrelling
with the Crown than in his old.

It is hard to see if Bacon were moved by personal
ambition, the public good, or a desire to annoy Coke.
Probably he was influenced by all three, for he and
Coke had long been acknowledged enemies. As
early as 1601 the two men had had a public row in the
House of Commons. Bacon's own account of it
makes Coke the aggressor, but one can imagine that
Bacon's scornful silence must have been extremely
exasperating to his bullying senior.

" I moved to have a reseizure of the lands of Geo. Moore, a relapsed recusant, a fugitive, and a practising traytor . . .

" Mr. Attorney kindled at it, and said, ' Mr. Bacon, if you have any tooth against me pluck it out, for it will do you more hurt than all the teeth in your head will do you good.' I answered coldly in these very words : ' Mr. Attorney, I respect you ; I fear you not ; and the less you speak of your own greatness the more I shall think of it.'

" He replied, ' I think scorn to stand upon terms of greatness towards you, who are less than little less than the least,' and other such strange light terms he gave me, with that insulting which cannot be expressed.

" Herewith stirred, yet I said no more but this : ' Mr. Attorney, do not depress me so far : for I have been your better, and may be again when it please the Queen.' "

The quarrel was so well-established that Bacon declared that he could never serve as Solicitor so long as Coke was Attorney, and no one had any doubt that it was Bacon who now caused Coke's undesired elevation. Coke reproached Bacon with the deed.

" Mr. Attorney, this is all your doing : it is you that have made this stir." To which Bacon answered in a jibe that has rather lost its savour.

" Ah, my Lord, your Lordship all this while hath grown in bredth ; you must needs now grow in height, or else you would be a monster."

But Bacon was the stronger force and Coke went to his new post lamentably enough. " On Monday the Lord Coke (though never so loth) was called up into the King's Bench, and there sworn Chief Justice.

He parted dolefully from the Common Pleas, not only weeping himself but followed with the tears of all the bench, and most of the officers of that court."

If Bacon hoped that Coke would learn wisdom, he was mistaken. At the King's Bench he was as troublesome as at the Common Pleas. He was fighting for an independent judiciary who, by balancing themselves between the contending parties of King and Parliament, would in effect be able to rule England. But unfortunately for Coke his pretensions were not to be allowed. The King lost patience, and an attack on the jurisdiction of the Court of Chancery alienated yet more feelings. Coke, having been brought before the Council, was suspended from his office and told to review his Reports to see if he had inserted in them views which were untenable.

This did not take place till just after the trial given in the next chapter, for Coke was still on the bench when Somerset was being tried, but it followed so soon after that the story cannot well be broken.

Coke's reply to this order to examine his Reports was magnificent. Summoned before the Lord Chancellor Ellesmere, Bacon the Attorney and all the learned counsel, he was told to give an " account of the performance of a commandment of His Majesty laid upon him, which was that he should enter into a view and retraction of such novelties and errors and offensive conceits as were dispersed in his Reports." To which Coke replied that in his Reports were " eleven books that contained about 500 cases " and in looking diligently through these he had detected four errors—all of the most trivial nature.

So bold an answer, which dared the King to do his worst, provoked anxious correspondence between

James and Bacon. Francis was for giving Coke a regular trial before the Council and the judges. He would then have had the full benefit of law, the whole matter would have been made public and the world would have known the reasons for the Government's action. James considered this method too slow, and after some consideration went straight to the point and used the power which he undoubtedly possessed of dismissing Coke himself.

Thus Coke received a curt notification: "For certain causes now moving us, we will that you shall be no longer our chief justice to hold the pleas before us, and we command you, that you no longer interfere in that office, and by virtue of this presence, we at once remove and exonerate you from this office."

Bacon's boast of fifteen years ago had come true— for a time. Coke, however, lived to win the last round in the game.

Chapter XIV

THE FALL OF SOMERSET

IN 1616 occurred one of the great cases of the age, a case which has remained a *cause célèbre* down to the present day and which ultimately interested Bacon in two ways : as Attorney General he had the chief management of it in court, and its result led to the establishment of Villiers as the King's chief favourite. It was the trial of Robert Carr, by that time Earl of Somerset, for the murder of Thomas Overbury by poison in the Tower.

The origin of the story is remote. In January, 1606, the young Earl of Essex, son of Elizabeth's favourite, married the still younger Frances Howard. It was a boy and girl marriage and the children were separated on the wedding day, the boy to travel on the Continent and the girl to lead the life of a court beauty ; so that the marriage, which was celebrated with festivities, masques, dances and feasting, was never consummated. When some six years later Essex returned to claim his bride, she was not only without affection for him, but had definitely bestowed her heart elsewhere. He carried her off to the country in the hope that she would find him more attractive when deprived of other amusements. She retorted by sulking, and finally petitioned for a divorce on the grounds of her husband's impotence. The truth was that she had long been Somerset's mistress, and they were determined to be married as soon as the impediment of the infantile contract could be removed. There being at the time no simple highway of divorce, the whole civil law of England must be disordered to free the Countess from a contract to which she had never really assented. Nor could the comparatively decent medical evidence of today be called, with the result that " the attention of the people of England was fixed on a transaction in which the parties were the somewhat incongruous personages of a king, bishops, doctors of civil law, matrons and midwives. The females of this junto were directed to examine whether the Countess of Essex appeared to their eyes, when disrobed, to be still a virgin ; whilst their royal, right-reverend, and learned associates were to decide, according to the verdict of the matrons, whether the lady had shown any adequate cause for divorce. King James not only sanctioned the proceedings, but impatiently urged them on and dictated their final conclusion."

The women decided in accordance with the King's wishes, but whether the matrons conducted their examination in a cursory fashion, or whether some more virtuous damsel, her face heavily veiled, was allowed to substitute for the Countess, is uncertain.

The further court was not left without guidance, as the following letter from the King to the Archbishop of Canterbury, who was recalcitrant, shows.

" I will conclude, therefore, that if a judge should have a prejudice in respect of persons, it should become you rather to have a *faith implicit* in my judgment, as well in respect of some skill I have in *divinity*, as also that I hope no honest man doubts of the uprightness of my conscience. And the best thankfulness that you that are so far *my creature* can

use towards me is to reverence and follow my judgment, and not contradict it, except where you may
demonstrate unto me that I am mistaken or wrongly
informed. And so farewell. JAMES R."

In fact, the Countess of Essex was in the same
position as Raleigh's estate of Sherborne. The King
" maun ha' her, maun ha' her for Carr ".

Have her he did, with two protesting voices, the
Archbishop of Canterbury who, being the King's
" creature ", suffered for his obstinacy by spending
the rest of his life in disgrace, and Thomas Overbury
who soon found himself in the Tower.

Overbury had been compared to Raleigh for pride ;
he was not his equal in literary genius, and thus we
have not his side of the case preserved and cherished.
His *Characters* read like the work of a bad-tempered,
sharp-tongued and dissolute man. He has much more
to say about whores than good women. Elder
brothers are his abominations and a Puritan " is a
diseased piece of Apocrypha : bind him to the
Bible and he corrupts the whole text ". Almost the
only pleasant character is the one regularly quoted of
the " *Faire and happy milk-mayd* ", and to the makers
of anthologies it shines brighter with its lambs and
spring flowers than it does to the readers, who do not
see it against a background of stews, prisons and dirty
raillery.

For several years Carr and Overbury had been
inseparable. Overbury's literary abilities must have
been invaluable to the less educated Scotsman, and at
an earlier stage it was Overbury's pen that framed
sonnets to Frances' beauty. But when Carr actually
proposed to marry the lady, Overbury was alarmed.
An alliance with the Howards would throw Carr into

ROBERT CARR, EARL OF SOMERSET

quite another faction, and it seems that while Overbury publicly insulted the Countess, he privately threatened Carr with the disclosure of sundry state secrets. Overbury's pen was sharp and he won the hatred of the Countess; his threats were really serious and he moved Carr to both fear and anger, with the result that very shortly Overbury was in the Tower on a trumped-up pretext, and then, not long after, he died painfully, with symptoms strongly suggesting arsenical poisoning.

Had all continued well with the fortunes of Somerset, the matter would probably have ended there, but James was growing tired of him, and Somerset's good fortune had unsettled his own judgment as to what a favourite might do. It is probable that a man in Somerset's position had better not be married, unless he possesses a wife more discreet and compliant than the Countess. Villiers managed to have a wife and retain the King's favour, but the sequence of events suggests that James's demands were such as to clash with those of the more orthodox expectations of the lady, and that Somerset preferred his honour to expediency. Moreover, interested persons had just invested their money and their favour in a newcomer. It was in those times as honourable to be a King's minion as to be his mistress, and the syndicate who took up young George Villiers, changed his threadbare clothes for court dress and purchased him the post of cupbearer, were acting in exactly the same way as those who introduced a new lady to the court of Louis XIV, and they hoped for as substantial a return on their investment.

The next stage in the proceedings can be best told by James himself, and the evidence is a letter to

Somerset which must have been written about this time. The letter consists of about seven pages of expostulation, pleading and attack, and taken in all is about as despicable a composition, as weak in thought and muddled in syntax, as ever came from a royal pen.

Somerset had considered himself suspected, but there he had erred. The King had no doubts, nor intended any diminution of favour towards him, yet he must complain :

" In those points I confess I never saw any come towards your merit : I mean, in the points of an inwardly trusty friend and servant. But, as a piece of ground cannot be so fertile, but if either by the own natural rankness or evil manuring thereof it become also fertile of strong and noisome weeds, it then proves useless and altogether unprofitable ; even so, these before rehearsed rich and rare parts and merits of yours have been of long time, but especially of late, since the strange phrenzy took you, so powdered and mixed with strange streams of unquietness, passion, fury, and insolent pride, and (which is worst of all) with a settled kind of induced obstinacy, as it chokes and obscures all those excellent and good parts."

And this mood had appeared in words. Late at night the King and Somerset quarrelled, and their voices, as well as the King's heavy looks next morning, apprised the court how things stood. Somerset had railed at him with " the tongue of the devil ".

" For, first, being uttered at unseasonable hours, and so bereaving me of my rest, was so far from condemning your own indiscretion therein, as by the contrary it seemed you did it of purpose to grieve

and vex me.   Next your fiery boutades were coupled
with a continual dogged sullen behaviour, especially
shortly after you fall and in all the times of your other
diseases.   Thirdly, in all your dealings with me, you
have many times uttered a kind of distrust of the
honesty of my friendship towards you.   And, fourthly
(which is worst of all), and worse than any other thing
that can be imagined, you have, in many of your mad
fits, done what you can to persuade me that you mean
not so much to hold me by love as by awe, and that
you have me so far in your reverence, as that I dare
not offend you, or resist your appetites.   I leave out of
this reckoning your long creeping back and withdrawing yourself from lying in my chamber, notwithstanding
my many times earnestly soliciting you to the contrary,
accounting that but a point of unkindness."

The matter is really serious.   " I protest in the
presence of Almighty God that I have borne this grief
within me to the uttermost of my ability ; neither
can I bear it longer without committing an unpardon-
able sin against God in consuming myself wilfully,
and not only myself, but in perilling thereby not only
the good estate of my own people, but even the state
of Religion through all Christendom, which almost
wholely, under God, rests now upon my shoulders."

And then the remedy.   " What shall be the best
remedy for this, I will tell you—be kind.   All I crave
is that in all the words and actions of your life you
may ever make it appear to me that you never think
to hold grip of me but out of my mere love, and not
one hair by force.   Consider that I am a free man, if
I were not a king."

This fine sentence leads on to the threat : " I had
rather have a conformable man with but ordinary

parts than the rarest man in the world that will not be obedient; for that leaven of pride sours the whole loaf.

"It lies in your hands to make of me what you please—either the best master and truest friend, or if you force me once to call you ingrate, which the God of heaven forbid, no so great earthly plague can light on you."

It might be possible to pity James in his rôle of maltreated lover, if it were not fairly certain that his eye had already lighted on the enchanting and effeminate form of young George Villiers; and did we not know that in a few months he would be kissing his cheeks and smoothing the folds of his garments. The person who really deserves sympathy, if there is any sympathy for such a depraved set, is Somerset, who, when once his rival was fairly in power, could expect nothing but destruction. With things in this pass, it is not remarkable that someone should come upon evidence tending to show that Overbury was murdered by Carr. The apothecary's boy, who had been employed to carry the powders, babbled, and those who wanted to ensure the good regard of Villiers carried the news to the King.

The crime was now two years old, and Somerset and his wife may well have felt safe. But first Weston, the under-keeper who had helped to administer the poison, then a Mrs. Turner who had supplied love-philtres to the Countess and later tested drugs, administering them to rabbits to see if they were quick or slow in action, were tried, condemned and executed. The woman was quaintly condemned to be hanged in a yellow starched ruff on the ground that she had introduced the fashion, and the judge, not

liking it, wished it might perish with her. All the
evidence pointed beyond these two and at Somerset
and his lady, who, apparently, had most to gain by
Overbury's death. There was little difficulty in
proving that the Countess was guilty. Somerset had
been more discreet, and evidence against him was
scanty; and yet all might have been well but for
Coke.

It was before this impetuous lawyer that the
earlier cases had come, and one day, the court being
met, Weston refused to plead. At that time a man
who refused was not assumed to plead " Not Guilty ";
he was sent back to prison, subjected to the *peine forte
et dure* till he either died or decided to stand his trial.
Weston did the latter after a few days' consideration,
but to fill up the time and avoid disappointing the
audience, Coke arranged, or at any rate sanctioned, a
statement in court in which there was " openly and at
large read the confession of the said Richard Weston,
and the testimonies of others, as well concerning the
fact of the said Richard Weston as the Earl and
Countess of Somerset, and Mrs. Turner, without
sparing any of them, or omitting anything material
against them ".

Not content with this, Coke continued to make
announcements from the bench of the magnitude of
the danger through which the state had passed.
" Knowing as much as he knew, if this plot had not
been found out, neither court, city, nor many particular houses had escaped the malice of that wicked
crew ", or " Our deliverance is as great as any that
happened to the children of Israel." Naturally
public opinion was afire, and expected not only a
glorious scandal, but complete proof of the guilt of

Somerset and his wife, who were commonly regarded as the principals in the plot. In this state the case came into Bacon's hands, who at once discovered that Coke's evidence was nought, being merely tales told by a man under sentence of death in an attempt to prolong his life; and that the most material part of it was hearsay and supposition of a kind that could not possibly be put to a jury with any hope of convincing them. At the same time the general opinion was that Somerset was certainly guilty, and his wife had confessed. Bacon must in his official capacity present the case for the Crown, and to do this temperately and yet successfully taxed all his ingenuity. His first letter to the King shows his doubts.

" I said to your Majesty that which I do now repeat, that the evidence upon which my Lord of Somerset standeth indicted is of a good strong thread, but that the thread must be well spun and woven together. For your Majesty knoweth it is one thing to deal with a jury of Middlesex and Londoners, and another to deal with the Peers, whose objects perhaps will not be so much what is before them in the present case (which I think is as odious to them as to the vulgar) but what may be hereafter. Besides, there be two disadvantages we that shall give in evidence shall meet with, somewhat considerable. The one, that the same things often opened leese their freshness, except there be an aspersion of somewhat that is new. The other is the expectation raised that make things seem less than they are, because they are less than opinion."

Further, when Bacon came to look into the evidence which had seemed to Coke adequate proof of guilt, it was all beside the point, and proved nothing.

There was one further complication, and that afforded by Somerset, who practically dared the King to bring him to trial, threatening that he would disclose secrets that would disgrace him. It was the same attitude that the King complained of in the letter already quoted, and though King and lawyers were extremely nervous, the King, remembering that he were a free man if he were not a king, held on his course.

It was no wonder, therefore, that anxious letters passed between the King and Bacon, discussing what they should do in a number of eventualities. They both prayed that Somerset might be induced to confess, then he could be spared even the ignominy of the trial and simply disappear quietly from public life.

To get this confession they were prepared to go considerable lengths, and they proposed sending someone to visit him in the Tower who would " unofficially " remind him of the King's favour to prisoners who confessed their guilt, and urge his adoption of the penitent role. Bacon puts it delicately yet definitely.

" The glimmering of that which the King hath done to others by way of talk to him cannot hurt as I conceive ; but I would not have that part of the message as from the King, but added by the messenger as from himself.

" For the person, though he trust the Lieutenant well, yet it must be some new man ; for in these cases, that which is ordinary worketh not so great an impression as that which is new and extraordinary.

" The time I wish to be the Tuesday, being the even of his Lady's arraignment. For, as his Majesty first conceived, I would not have it stay in his stomach too

long, lest it sour in the digestion ; and to be too near
the time may be thought but to tune him for that day."

But Somerset was firm, and though the Countess
pleaded guilty, and was dismissed with tender words
by Bacon, he refused to relieve King or prosecutor
of his anxieties.

Bacon's management of the case when it came into
court was a masterpiece of ingenuity. Above everything else he wished to avoid driving Somerset to
despair or exasperation, so that he should be tempted
to turn on the King and either make charges against
him or, if that were actually prevented, produce an
ill impression in court or among people at large. At
the same time he must show a case for conviction, and
express the horror which he and everybody else felt
for the crime of poisoning. " For impoisonment (he
said in court) I am sorry it should be heard of in this
kingdom : it is not *nostri generis nec sanguinis :* it is
an Italian crime, fit for the court of Rome . . ."
And indeed the English Renaissance is singularly
free from this crime that made every tyrant's life
unsafe, and threatened every unwanted brother in
other lands.

Bacon speaks of poisoning as a singularly base
crime, but he speaks generally. Somerset was accused
of it, and yet the speech is as general as if Bacon were
delivering a lecture, and his illustrations are from Cain
and Abel, not from more moving topics. Then he
proceeds to point out that his evidence is mainly of
motive and circumstantial.

" Your Lordships must consider that impoisonment
of offences is the most secret : so secret, as if in all
cases of impoisonment you should require testimony,
you were as good proclaim impunity." Therefore he

will show that Somerset had reason to kill Overbury, that he took steps that would facilitate the killing, that he later behaved as a guilty man might be expected to behave. Finally he would show some indications that Somerset actually did it, or at least helped to do it, but on this point he promises little, and it remained the weakest part of the case.

In showing the motive, Bacon is again admirably astute. Overbury was dead. No one had cared for him, and though it does not excuse a murder to say that the victim was an odious person, it certainly puts the accused in an easier position, and is less likely to provoke an outbreak. So Overbury is represented as an overbearing blackmailer, and Somerset's anxiety to get him out of the way becomes so natural as to be a potent argument for his guilt.

Then follows an account of the steps which led to Overbury's imprisonment, the special arrangements which were made for his keeping, and the tale of his death. The final section was the conduct of Somerset when he began to fear discovery. First he had tried to get a general pardon from the King covering a host of crimes, including poisoning. This had been stopped, then when he saw accusations drawing in on him he had used the last of his power to seize and destroy papers and had had others mutilated and misdated.

Somerset had been provided with pen and ink to make notes for his answer, and was told that he could have all the time he wished. He began well, admitted his hatred of Overbury, but denied that that hate led to murder. He had no need to prove that he did not poison Overbury; the evidence was too slight to show that he did. It was when he came to answer the last part of the evidence that he broke down. He *had* destroyed and falsified evidence, and he could give no reason why.

The jury, after a long consultation, were unanimous in their verdict of " Guilty ". Bacon, King and court heaved a sigh of relief. Justice was satisfied by the disgrace of the great. The poor who had furthered the plot had nothing to lose but their lives, so they perished. Somerset and his wife suffered civil death, but continued to breathe the air. Indeed, the Countess, in accordance with the half-promise held out to her at her trial, was pardoned, and it was Bacon who drew the document. He did it as an official duty, but probably he did it with pleasure for his nature had no savagery in it. They were both released from the Tower in 1622 and allowed to live in certain fixed places.

CHAPTER XV

LORD CHANCELLOR

SOMERSET'S disgrace left the way clear for Villiers, and the men about the court were not slow to welcome him. Among others he received greetings from the Archbishop of Canterbury, who had such good reason for preferring the rising to the setting favourite.

> And now, my George, because of your kind affection towards me, you style me your father. I will from this day forward respect and esteem you for my son, and so hereafter know yourself to be. And in token thereof, I do now give you my blessing again, and charge you as my son, daily to serve God, to be diligent and pleasing to your master, and to be wary that, at no man's instance, you press him with many suits ; because they are not your friends that urge those things upon you, but have private ends of their own, which are not fit for you. So praying God to bless you, I rest
>
> Your very loving father,
G. CANT.
>
> Lambeth, 10th December, 1615.
> To my very loving son, Sir George Villiers,
>   Knight and Gentleman of his Majestie's Bedchamber.

Thus greeted, thus fathered by the church, Villiers was not slow in rising to the place, almost the office, of acknowledged favourite. He was young, ignorant, half-educated. He was later to display the greatest incompetence in everything he undertook, and his murder was to be received with a universal sigh of satisfaction. But he had the gifts to catch James's eye and the power to hold his affection. He was colossally selfish, but good-natured. He managed to maintain a certain dignity when he wrote to Bacon,

and with the King he corresponded in an odious
mixture of servility and impudence, addressing James
as " Dere Dad and gossope " and signing himself
" Your Majestie's humble slave and doge, Steenie."
But he came in with a fair wind, and spoke everyone
well. He might even have been following Bacon's
own precept to " apply his questions to the skill of
the person of whom he asketh ", for he wrote to
Bacon asking advice on matters of state, and was
answered by a treatise on the whole condition of the
realm. Not content with thus instructing the favourite in general politics, Bacon wrote to him pointing out
his duty in his new position, and the dangers to which
he would be exposed. No letter could be less that
of a flatterer. It is rather calculated in its cold discussion of dangers and duties to produce a chill in an
ardent youth about to start on a glorious career.

" Sir, in the first place, I shall be bold to put you
in mind of the present condition you are in. You are
not only a courtier, but a bed-chamber-man, and so are
in the eye and ear of your master ; but you are also a
Favourite, the Favourite of the time, and so are in his
bosom also. The world hath so voted you, and doth
so esteem you ; for kings and great princes, even the
wisest of them, have had their friends, their favourites,
their privadoes, in all ages ; for they have their
affections as well as other men. Of these they make
several uses ; sometimes to communicate and debate
their thoughts with them, and to ripen their judgments
thereby ; sometimes to ease their cares by imparting
them ; and sometimes to interpose them between
themselves and the envy or malice of their people.
(For kings cannot err ; that must be discharged on
the shoulders of their ministers, and they who are

nearest unto them must be content to bear the greatest load.) Truly, Sir, I do not believe or suspect that you are chosen to this eminency out of the last of these considerations. But I am confident his Majesty hath cast his eyes upon you as finding you to be such as you should be, or hoping to make you to be such as he would have you to be ; for this I may say without flattery, your outside promiseth as much as can be expected from a gentleman. But be it in one respect or another, it belongeth to you to take care of yourself, and to know well what the name of Favourite signifies. If you be chosen upon the former respects, you have reason to take care of your actions and deportment, out of your gratitude, for the King's sake ; but if out of the latter, you ought to take the greater care for your own sake. You are as a new-risen star, and the eyes of all men are upon you : let not your own negligence make you fall like a meteor . . ."

Villiers certainly had the power to adapt his manners to his company, and while he baptized pigs for James's diversion, managed to behave to Bacon, for the greater part of his life, somewhat in the tone of this letter. But Bacon in his turn knew very well the manner which even the greatest officer of the realm ought to adopt to a Favourite. After all, as Attorney or even as Lord Chancellor, he is but a servant of the King, and the King's favourite takes precedence over the greatest servant. So that from now on his letters to Villiers (or Buckingham) join him in glorious unity with the King, and to each of these foolish beings Bacon expresses the deepest devotion and submission.

" Thus your Lordship may see my love and care towards you, which I think infinitely too little in respect of the fullness of my mind ; but I thought good to write this, to make you understand better the state of your own business ; doing by you as I do by the King, which is to do his business safely and with foresight not only of tomorrow or the next day, but afar off, and not to come fiddling with a report to him what is done every day, but to give him a good sum in the end."

In the same way when he has written out an opinion on a legal point—perhaps consulted with the judges— he always ends : " All which nevertheless I in all humbleness submit to your Majestie's better judgment."

The strange thing again is that Bacon was sincere. He held himself truly a servant of the crown ; he boasted that he had never received rebuke from his master ; he held himself due to give to the monarch all counsel, care and obedience. He offered the best advice that he could devise, and if this were not accepted, devoted all his intelligence to making the method chosen successful. He was the perfect Civil Servant and he prided himself on being it. He does not seem ever to have felt insulted by his treatment, ever to have noticed a discrepancy between his acts and his conscience, ever to have wearied in the discharge of business. He contrived to serve both his God and his King, and as Buckingham for many purposes was the King, he served him, too, as faithfully as the others.

He was, moreover, grown very great. He could claim the highest offices in the state and be granted them, even though he plainly announced that he would not pay the King the usual bribes for their granting.

When Yelverton became Attorney General, he paid the King £4,000 for the post ; and James on receiving it threw his arms round the new Attorney General and gave thanks that he could now buy some dishes, of which he was very much in want.

Bacon, writing to solicit the Chancellorship, adopts a very different tone. Ellesmere was dying, and this is how Bacon asks for the promise of the place :

" It may please your most excellent Majesty, your worthy Chancellor, I fear, goes his last day. God hath hitherto used to weed out such servants as grew not fit for your Majesty. But now he hath gathered to himself a true safe, or salvia, out of your garden. But your Majesty's service must not be mortal . . .

" I shall now again make oblation to your Majesty, first of my heart, then of my service, thirdly of my place of Attorney, which I think is honestly worth £6,000 per annum, and fourthly of my place of the Star Chamber, which is worth £1,600 per annum, and with the favour and countenance of a Chancellor much more . . ."

By all this Bacon means that if he is given the Chancellorship he will have to vacate his two other posts, and the King can then sell them for what they will fetch, and he will do his best to make the purchaser pleased with his bargain. Another man would have offered the King a bribe in addition, or have tried to make something himself on the offices he was resigning. Under a King who regularly sold the offices of state for services of plate, Bacon behaved according to the modern standard of probity.

But though he offered no gift (and his rival tendered £30,000) his position was such that he was promised the Chancellorship, and on Ellesmere's final resignation he received the great seal at once without further canvass.

Thus quietly, easily, Bacon achieved the goal on which his eyes had been set during the whole of his official life. He had been destined for this office in his cradle, had been chaffed about it when he was a grave-faced small boy walking with his father in the gardens of the Great Queen, had dreamed about it all the long years of patient service. When Robert Cecil died he had begun to feel freedom and hope, when his scheming made him Attorney General that hope must have been transformed into confidence. All the days of Ellesmere's long illness he watched with real friendship and devotion for the dying man, but also considering what he could do to strengthen his own position. He had longed for this office as for a bride, and as a bride he received it, with pomp in public, and in private with a brevity of thankfulness that makes his style completely simple.

To my Lord of Buckingham

My dearest Lord,

It is both in cares and kindness, that small ones float up to the tongue, and great ones sink down into the heart with silence. Therefore, I could speak little to your Lordship to-day, neither had I fit time : but I must profess this much, that in this day's work you are the truest and perfectest mirror and example of firm and generous friendship that ever was in court ; and I shall count every day lost, wherein I shall not either study your well doing in thought, or do your name honour in speech, or perform your service in deed. Good, my Lord, account and accept me, your most boundless and devoted friend and servant of all men living.

Fr. Bacon C.S.

If this was the thanks of his heart to Buckingham, his public glory waited two months, till May 7th, the first day of the new term ; and then he rode in state to take his seat in Westminster Hall. The King was already on his journey to Scotland, with Buckingham and the court, and Bacon was the greatest man in England. With that love of display and sense of drama which distinguished one side of his nature, he rode to his second bridal dressed all in purple velvet as he had ridden to his first eleven years before. It was the same high spring weather and the route past Whitehall lay largely through gardens. The buildings were irregular and scattered, and the famous banqueting hall, from which Charles I stepped to the scaffold, had not yet been begun. The procession was carefully ordered : " (1) Clerks and inferior officers in Chancery, (2) students in Law, (3) Gentlemen, servants of the Lord Keeper, serjeants at arms and the seal bearer, all on foot, (4) Himself on horseback in a gown of purple sattin, between the Lord Treasurer and the Keeper of the Privy Seal, (5) Earls, Barons, Privy Councillors, (6) Noblemen of all ranks, (7) Judges to whom the next place to the Privy Councillors was assigned." Behind them again came " the nobility and other gallants to the number of more than 200 horses. There was a great deal more bravery and better show of horses than was expected in the King's absence ; but both the Queen and Prince sent all their followers, and his other friends did their best to honour him."

Thus in sunshine and brilliant clothes, with clatter of bits and stirrups they came to Westminster Hall, and Bacon took his Judge's seat in that hall of noble proportions, while the angels looked down on him from the hammer beams of its forested roof. He sat enthroned above the deep flights of steps, and the sides and body of the hall were packed with the

brilliantly clad crowd that had come to enjoy the
ceremony and congratulate the highest official in
the Kingdom.

To this audience Bacon made his speech, explaining
the principles on which he was going to govern his
rather troubled realm of Chancery. The different
heads of his speech indicate fairly the main problems
which he saw before him.

The first was the conflict of jurisdiction, between
Chancery and the courts of Common Law. In this
matter, while maintaining the pre-eminence of the
Chancery, he would be careful not to go beyond his
own sphere, and would vigorously discourage suitors
who attempted to play off one court against another,
or to use Chancery as a means of delaying justice.

As regards delay, which was the curse of the court,
he intended to work afternoons as well as mornings,
and to take some weeks from the vacations. " Only
the depth of the three long vacations ", he said, " I
would reserve in some measure free for business of
estate, and for studies, arts and sciences, to which in
my nature I am most inclined."

Further he would always give his decisions promptly
but only after patient hearing of the case, and in such
a form that they were not likely to be questioned
afterwards.

Lastly, as to excessive charges, he would do what
he could by expedition, since delays were the cause of
most expense. Further, he would cut down the
" needless prolixity and length of bills ", shorten
depositions, and see that fees be on the standard
scale.

After Bacon's speech the courtiers departed, but
the lawyers were invited to stay on and hear the first

FRANCIS BACON, LORD CHANCELLOR

[face p. 172

case. Unfortunately it did not go well, for the young lawyer who had been granted the honour of moving the first motion had not prepared his speech properly and disgraced himself, so that his friends were driven to make excuses for him, and Bacon felt upset.

This lack of success a little marred the glory of the day, but the slip was repaired in the evening. The dinner which Bacon gave to his followers cost £700, and he took the first step in promoting good will between himself and the judges of the Common Law by inviting them all to a special banquet at which over gold and silver plates, roasted swans and pea-cocks, and exotic fruit the cause of legal harmony flourished.

What Bacon himself thought as he rode in state is recorded in a letter he sent to Buckingham the next day.

"Yesterday I took my place in Chancery. There was much ado, and a great deal of world. But this matter of pomp, which is heaven to some men, is hell to me, or purgatory at least. It is true I was glad to see that the King's choice was so generally approved, and that I had so much interest in men's good wills and good opinions, because it maketh me the fitter instrument to do my master service and my friend also."

The last half sentence is written as the courtier, but the first part of the paragraph doubtless tells the truth ; though one is left to conjecture whether it were a kind of deep shyness, or a sense of the worthlessness of forms that made it purgatory for Bacon to ride in procession on a fine May morning.

To the work of the court Bacon devoted himself with enthusiasm ; and his powers of expedition were marvellous. Probably his own natural ability was the determining factor. He saw the point of a case at once, and decided immediately. His predecessor had been in the habit of reserving judgment and of not pronouncing a decree for months after hearing the case. Bacon never did that, and he not only worked in the afternoons, but summoned many of the parties to his own house to hear them in private and more expeditiously than he could have done in court. Many of the cases were long and tiresome in the extreme, and came to Bacon after decisions in the Common Law Courts which had been disliked by one of the parties. We know the details of a few of them because they were revived when he was accused of corruption.

One of the cases which Bacon inherited from his predecessor concerned a will. Edward Egerton in return for financial assistance had conveyed to his relative, Sir John Egerton, his lands, and especially his estate of Wrynehill in Staffordshire. Sir John had a son Rowland who was married. When Sir John died in 1614 it was found that after making provision for his widow he had left the rest of his estate to the spendthrift Edward Egerton. Whereupon Rowland appealed to Chancery for redress. It was found that a few years before his death Sir John had executed a deed conveying to the trustees of his son's marriage settlement a large part of his estate, including Wryne-hill. The decision was that this deed took precedence over the will, and therefore Rowland could claim the land disposed of by it; and as to the rest, the will must be investigated and, till that were done, each party should remain in possession of the lands which his father had owned.

Rowland was apparently contented having the best of the bargain ; but Edward, being excluded from Wrynehill, which he loved, resisted the division of lands by every means in his power, and attempted to get hold of the deed by which he had originally conveyed Wrynehill to Sir John. So Bacon found the case, and one of his first acts was to resist Edward's application for the deed. All documents were to remain in court till the validity of the will was settled, and this settlement would not be made in Chancery. Therefore Bacon felt that the case was finished so far as concerned himself.

He was now furnishing York House and was receiving a stream of presents, so when Edward Egerton arrived with a bag containing £400 no one was surprised—except at the size of the gift. Bacon weighed the bag in his hand and said it was more than he cared to receive, so he sent it back again by the hand of Sir Richard Young who had received it. The bag was returned with an assurance that it was a gift for past services, and so Bacon accepted it, and put it aside with the polite message that the donor " had not only enriched him, but had laid a tie on him to do him justice in all his rightful causes ".

But the contending parties would not let the matter rest here. A month or two later the will was pronounced valid, but the parties quarrelled again and asked Bacon to act as arbitrator. This he did ; and decided, in accordance with the law, that two-thirds of the lands not already conveyed to the trustees of the marriage settlement should go to Edward and this remaining third to Rowland. Edward refused to accept this decision : so long as Rowland had Wrynehill he would never be quiet, and Bacon had to hear the case again as a formal suit and reaffirm his arbitrator's decision by a binding decree.

Edward was still not satisfied, and taking advantage of the state of the law he transferred his suit to the King's Bench—and lost again. He therefore regarded Bacon with mortal hatred.

But in spite of all these difficulties Bacon's industry and clear-headedness were such that he cleared off the arrears of cases in the court. Within the month he could write jubilantly to Buckingham :

" This day I have made even with the business of the Kingdom for common justice. Not one case unheard. The lawyers drawn dry of all the motions they were to make. Not one petition unanswered, and this I think could not be said in our age before. This I speak not out of ostentation, but out of gladness, when I have done my duty. I know men think I cannot continue, if I should thus oppress myself with business. But that account is made. The duties of life are more than life. And if I die now I shall die before the world is weary of me, which in our times is somewhat rare."

This is surely the only occasion on record when a highly-placed civil servant has been level with his work.

CHAPTER XVI

COKE AND HIS DAUGHTER

WITH the King and Buckingham away in Scotland, Bacon as Lord Chancellor was governor of England. The post was, however, far from peaceful. It was not the law business of Chancery, nor the ordinary routine of government which disturbed him; it was not the stately parade of entertaining foreign ambassadors; a personal row brought down on him perplexity and court anger. Coke, deprived of his Chief Justiceship, languished; and, casting about for means to restore himself, took up again a bargain with Buckingham which greed on both sides had prevented from being accomplished in the days of his prosperity.

John Villiers, elder brother of the favourite, was unprovided for, and it had occurred to the scheming mother of these sons that Coke might be prepared to barter his daughter Frances and £10,000 for an assurance of court favour. Coke does not seem to have scrupled at all about his daughter, but at first he refused to go higher than £7,000 in money, and the negotiation was suspended, Lady Compton feeling that she had time on her side, as indeed she had. Coke, with no occupation, Parliament not sitting, and the odious sight of Bacon governing England before his eyes, at last decided that if £3,000 was all that stood between him and a public life he was a fool to

grudge it.   So he intimated to the Villiers party that
he was ready to agree to their terms, and the negotiation was resumed.   James was satisfied, Buckingham
eager ; poor Frances was not considered.   It remained
for Bacon to object on what he professed to be
reasons of state, and for Lady Hatton, Frances'
mother, to intervene in her usual high-handed way
and carry off her daughter to a house in the country.

Bacon could not allow the domestic feuds of these
very important people to go unwatched, nor could he
neglect what he believed to be the interest of the King
and Buckingham, but he in no way wished to interfere
beyond his own province ; so he wrote a letter to
Buckingham urging him to bid his brother do no more
about the match at least till the court was back in
London, and he could look into the matter himself.
" For ", says he, " this match, out of my faith and
freedom towards your Lordship, I hold very inconvenient both for your brother and yourself.

" First, he shall marry into a disgraced house, which
in reason of state is never good.

" Next, he shall marry into a troubled house of man
and wife, which in religion and Christian discretion
is disliked.

" Thirdly, your Lordship will go near to lose all
such your friends as are adverse to Sir Edward Coke
(myself only excepted, who out of a pure love and
thankfulness will always be faithful to you).

" And lastly and chiefly (believe it) it will greatly
weaken and distract the King's service ; for though, in
regard of the King's great wisdom and depth, I am
persuaded these things will not follow which they
imagine, yet opinion will do a great deal of harm,
and cast the King back, and make him relapse into

those inconveniences which are now well on to be recovered."

Before Buckingham could possibly answer this, the matter had gone to open violence between the parents. Coke, who for a Lord Chief Justice was one of the most illegal men in England (he had even managed to marry his wife in a manner contrary to regulation), went off with his son, " fighting Clem Coke ", and a rabble of armed servants, broke open the doors of the house where Frances was, and dragged his poor trembling daughter, aged only fourteen, to a coach—and so up to London.

Lady Hatton, scarcely more legal, had been beaten in her race with her husband, but had prepared herself " three score men and pistols " and a band of Lords to lead them, and was only prevented by the chance of not meeting her husband on the road as she expected from having a set battle.

Preserved by accident from an open brawl, she applied to the more pacific remedies of the law. She made straight for Bacon's house, " but could not have instant access to him for that his people told her he was laid at rest, being not well. Then my Lady Hatton desired she might be in the next room where my Lord lay, that she might be the first that should speak with him after he was stirring. The door-keeper fulfilled her desire and in the meantime gave her a chair to rest herself in, and there left her alone ; but not long after, she rose up and bounced against my Lord Keeper's door, and waked him and affrighted him, that he called his men to him ; and they opening the door, she thrust in with them, and desired his Lordship to pardon her boldness, but she was like a cow that had lost her calf, and so justified herself and pacified my Lord's anger, and got his warrant, and my Lord Treasurer's warrant, and others of the Council to fetch her daughter from the father and bring them both to the Council."

The Council, not knowing what to do between the two furious spouses, committed poor Frances to neutral custody, where she was importuned on the one hand by Lady Compton, proposer of the match, and by Lady Burleigh, her mother's partisan. Thus situated, she wrote to her mother as pathetic a letter as ever harassed fourteen-year-old penned.

" I resolve to be wholly ruled by my father and yourself, knowing your judgments to be such that I may well rely upon, and hoping that conscience and the natural affection parents bear to children will let you do nothing but for my good, and that you may receive comfort, I being a mere child, and not understanding the world nor what is good for myself. . . ." She only hoped that her marriage would do her father's position good, and might end in a peaceful settlement between her parents.

As to the bridegroom, whom she had barely seen, she could say little. Indeed there was little to be said, seeing that he was one of those men who must rely on a brother to provide him with any recommendation at all.

" For himself your ladyship is not to be misliked; his fortune is very good, a gentleman well born . . ."

And the final postscript suggests that, much as she had suffered, she had escaped the worst.

" P.S. Dear Mother, believe there hath no violent means been used to me, by words or deeds."

The Council could not allow the matter to rest there, but feeling that if the law were once publicly flouted

by a man as great as Coke, all lesser fathers might
think themselves justified in housebreaking in pursuit
of their daughters, it was determined to prefer an
information in the Star Chamber against Coke for
riot.   And so it would have been done, if a messenger
had not come from the North with a very different
view of the case.

The King could not see that it was a " matter of
noise and streperous carriage " for any father to hunt
for his child that had been stolen away from him, nor
could he bear that his Buckingham should be thwarted
in any way in a matter that he had set his heart upon.
He therefore intimated clearly to the Council that
Sir Edward Coke was in the right, and all proceedings
against him must stop.

That being so, the Council gave up law and justice,
and, taking on themselves the more amiable task of
peacemakers, got on so well that Coke, his wife and
daughter were all at home together again, prepared
to enjoy each other's society during a short truce in
their inter-family wars.

Bacon must have smiled a little grimly.   He had
once thought of courting Lady Hatton for her money,
but Coke had won her, and suffered her furious
temper ever since.   It was pleasant to think that a
successful rival had not gained too much by his
triumph.   But such satisfaction as this was short-
lived.   The court was angry, and during the leisurely
progress South Bacon wrote anxiously to the King
and Buckingham, pointing out that he had acted in
what he believed to be the interest of both the court
and the law, and that as soon as he was informed of
the royal will he had done everything in his power to
forward it.   The letters went unanswered, and when

Buckingham did condescend to write his letter was rude ; this first check to his omnipotence made him furious, and he had not yet learnt his later subtlety in enforcing submission.

To the Lord Keeper Bacon.

My Lord,

If your man had been addressed only to me, I should have been careful to have procured him a more speedy dispatch ; but now you have found another way of address, I am excused ; and since you are grown weary of employing me, I can be no otherwise in being employed. In this business of my brother's that you overtrouble yourself with, I understand from London by some of my friends that you have carried yourself with much scorn and neglect both towards myself and friends, which if it prove true I blame not you but myself, who was ever

Your Lordship's assured friend.

Bacon could not leave London to urge his own part, and had to rely on the reports which Yelverton, his friend and fellow councillor, sent him.

" My most worthy and honourable Lord,

Sir Edward Coke hath not forborn any engine to heave both at you honour and myself ; and he works by the weightiest instrument, the Earl of Buckingham, who as I see sets him as close to him as his shirt, the Earl speaking in Sir Edward's phrase, and as it were menacing in his spirit.

My Lord, I emboldened myself to assay the temper of my Lord of Buckingham to myself, and found it very fervent, misled by misinformation which yet I find he embraced as truth, and did nobly and plainly tell me that he would not secretly bite, but who-so-ever had had any interest or tasted of the opposition to his brother's marriage he would openly oppose them to their faces, and they should discern what favour he had by the power he would use.

ROBERT DEVEREUX, EARL OF ESSEX

[face p. 66

Now my Lord, give me leave out of all my affections that shall ever serve you, to intimate touching yourself :

1st.   That every courtier is acquainted that the Earl professeth openly against you as forgetful of his kindness, and unfaithful to him in your love and affections.

2nd.   That he returneth the shame upon himself in not listening to counsel that dissuaded his affection from you, and not to mount you so high, not forbearing in open speech to tax you, as if it were an inveterate custom with you, to be unfaithful to him as you were to the Earls of Essex and Somerset.

3rd.   That it is too common in everyman's mouth in court, that your greatness shall be abated, and as your tongue hath been as a razor to some, so shall theirs be to you.

4th.   That there be laid up for you, to make your burden the more grievous, many petitions to his Majesty against you."

The effect of this letter on Bacon can be easily guessed.   Barely six months Chancellor and involved in a matter which bid fair to lose him court favour altogether.   Buckingham and the King hostile.   Sir Edward Coke triumphing exceedingly " as if he were already upon his wings ", and the riffraff of politics eager to destroy the fallen.   But when the court was back in London about September 15th, and Bacon could put his own case, the quarrel rapidly healed. The reconciliation was perhaps helped by Bacon's fortunate discovery of one Baynton who in drink or madness uttered threats against the King's life, and thus gave Bacon an opportunity of again approaching his Sovereign in the capacity of a faithful and vigilant servant.

Something also touched Buckingham's heart, and he became gracious :

"I do freely confess that your offer of submission unto me, and in writing (if so I would have it) battered so the unkindness that I had conceived in my heart for your behaviour towards me in my absence, as out of the sparks of my old affection towards you I went to sound his Majesty's intention how he means to behave himself towards you specially in any public meeting ; where I found on the one part his Majesty so little satisfied with your late answer unto him, which he counted (for I protest, I use his own terms) confused and childish, and his vigorous resolution on the other part so fixed that he would put some public exemplary mark upon you, as I protest the sight of his deep conceived indignation quenched my passions, making me upon the instant change from the person of a part into a peace-maker ; so as I was forced upon my knees to beg of his Majesty that he would put no public act of disgrace upon you. . . . Only thus far his Majesty protesteth, that upon the conscience of his office he cannot omit (laying aside all passion) to give a kingly reprimand at his first sitting in council to so many of his councillors as were then here behind and were actors in this business, for their ill behaviour in it."

Bacon's relief when he received this letter was deep ; and his answer, if adapted to the recipient, was probably very nearly sincere.

"My ever best Lord, now better than yourself. Your Lordship's pen or rather pencil hath portrayed towards me such magnanimity and nobleness and true kindness, as methinks I see the image of some ancient virtue, and not anything of these times. It is the line

LETTER FROM FRANCIS BACON TO THE DUKE OF BUCKINGHAM

[face p. 184

of my life, and not the lines of my letter, that must express my thankfulness : wherein if I fail, then God fail me, and make me as miserable as I think myself at this time happy by this reviver, through his Majesty's singular clemency, and your incomparable love and favour.   God preserve you, prosper you, and reward you for your kindness to

Your raised and infinitely obliged friend or servant,

FRANCIS BACON, C.S."

So Bacon, who had been in the right all through, was forgiven, and the King's statement in the council was more a defence of his own conduct than a reproof, and ended with a piece of the unconscious blasphemy at which he excelled.

" I, James, am neither a god nor an angel, but a man like any other.   Therefore I act like a man, and confess to loving those dear to me more than other men.   You may be sure I love the Earl of Buckingham more than anyone else, and more than you who are here assembled.   I wish to speak in my own behalf, and not to have it thought to be a defect, for Jesus Christ did the same, and therefore I cannot be blamed. Christ had his John and I have my George."

Thus ended Bacon's part in the matter ; Frances was hastily married off to John Villiers whom she did not love and soon deserted ; Coke became a Privy Councillor again ; and Lady Hatton, after a period of resistance, gave a great banquet to indicate that she was willing after all to settle her fortune on her daughter's husband.

CHAPTER XVII

LIFE AT YORK HOUSE

BACON could scarce be Lord Chancellor and not live in York House. His father had lived there when he held the office, and there Francis had been born. Ellesmere had been its tenant till his resignation, and in five months after obtaining office Bacon was living there in the high tide of his glory. He loved the house, for old associations and for itself. It was quiet, beautiful, and its gardens and terraces above the river were a source of delight. No sooner had his hands touched it than he began to improve it. He was a constitutional builder, and before ever his lease was firmly settled he had spent a vast sum, nearly £6,000 of his own money, on repairs and renovations. Besides the structural renovations he had built himself an aviary at the cost of about £300 (in the money of the day) and stocked it with birds. One day a crane escaped and flew out to the Thames, only to be promptly recaptured by a washerwoman who was plying her trade on the steps that ran down to the river. The stately terraces of these noble houses must often have been decked with the household washing.

Within, the house was magnificently furnished. All his well-wishers sent him gifts, and many a suitor in Chancery whose case was settled, and indeed a few whose cases were not, added their offerings to swell

S PAULES CHURCH

THAMESIS

VIEW OF LONDON, 1616

[face p. 186

the tide of magnificence. Four hundred pounds was
a gift to buy a suit of hangings, a cabinet arrived
which the donor valued at £800. Poorer men sent
money for curtains and plate. Bacon among all this
liberality kept a royal state, accepting all and never
asking himself if any of the gifts which came so
abundantly were intended to influence his judgments
in court.

His own wealth he spent with an equal profusion.
He had never valued money save for the luxury and
beauty that it could purchase, and now he gave his
fancy full sway. With his love of rich stuffs and
gorgeous colours it is no wonder if his upholsterer's
bill amounted in four months to £647 7s. 6d.

In all details the house must be perfect. Some
rooms needed the richness of stained glass, others
where one retired to read must have fair wide windows
of clear crystalline glass. There must be ornaments
here and there to catch and amuse the eye. Especially
must there be balls of coloured glass and coloured
lanterns to cheer the mind by their cheerful brightness.
Bacon would not live without flowers. Not only did
they stand in his rooms to please him with their smell
as he went to and fro', but at every meal the table
must be strewn with them, so that their fragrance
might refresh his spirit and memory. Whenever he
could get them, his dinner blossoms were orange
flowers.

This side of life, in spite of all his public concerns,
was very important to him. He entered in his notebooks recipes for drying rose leaves, or for making a
cooling drink from pomegranates.

" The artificial preparation of Damask Roses for smell.

" Take roses, pull their leaves, then dry them in a

clear day, in the hot sun ; then their smell will be as gone. Then cram them into an earthen Bottle, very dry and sweet, and stop it very close ; they will remain in smell and colour both fresher, than those that are otherwise dried."

He would make himself fruit drinks for hot days.

" Take sweet Pomegranates, and strain them lightly, not pressing the Kernel, into a glass : where put some little of the peel of a citron, and two or three cloves, and three grains of amber-grease, and a pretty deal of fine sugar. It is to be drunk every morning whilst Pomegranates last."

Nor were the other senses uncared for. When he meditated, either thinking of his philosophy or the details of his official business, he would have music played in the adjoining room so that the notes came through to him softened.

He was particular about small matters.

" None of his servants durst appeare before him without Spanish leather bootes ; for he would smelle the neate leather which offended him."

Bacon's luxury was always of this type, a delicate perfecting of the art of life, and it never interfered with business. His occupation was continuous. This is his account of his week :

" Yesterday was a day of motions in the Chancery ; this day was a day of motions in the Star Chamber (and it was my hap to clear the bar, that no man was left to move any thing, which my Lords were pleased to note they never saw before) ; tomorrow is sealing day ; Thursday is the Funeral day (the Queen was dead) ; so I pray your Lordship to direct me whether I shall attend his Majesty Friday or Saturday. Friday hath some reliques of business, and the commissioners of treasure have appointed to meet, but to see his Majesty is to me above all."

The King chose Saturday for an interview, and on Sunday, after church, the Council met, so Bacon's week was quite full with set business.

In addition, there was a perpetual flow of diverse matters, patents to examine and seal, cases to consider, projects for improving the King's revenue to examine and report on. Most of the business is now uninteresting to us, but one letter contains a point of view that is interesting and shows difficulties in the foundation of one modern institution.

Alleyne, the actor who had created Marlow's great characters of *Tamberlaine* and *Faustus*, wished to leave his money to found Dulwich College. Bacon opposed it. "I now write to give the King an account of a patent I have stayed at the seal. It is a licence to give in mortmain eight hundred pound land, though it be a tenure in chief, to Allen that was a player, for an hospital.

"I like well that Allen playeth the last act of his life so well, but if his Majesty give way thus to amortize his tenures, his Court of Wards shall decay, which I had well hoped should improve.

"But that which moved me chiefly is, that his Majesty did absolutely deny Sir Henry Savile for £200 and Sir Edwin Sandys for £100 to the perpetuating of two lectures, the one in Oxford, the other in Cambridge, foundations of singular honour to his Majesty (the best learned of kings) and of which there is great want ; whereas hospitals abound, and beggars abound never a whit the less." Bacon's bitterness is probably due rather to the refusal of the University lectureships than to the thought of the encouragement to beggars.

Another incident shows us Bacon presiding at the Council table. The Earl of Suffolk had been guilty, as Lord Treasurer, of gross peculation and extortion and he was brought to the Star Chamber to answer the charges against him and be sentenced. As was the custom, the junior councillor spoke first, Bacon as president reserving his speech till the end.

" My Lord Chancellor to conclude (as his manner is) made an eloquent speech in praise of his Majesty and the present Government : that his Majesty was an uniter and planter of kingdoms ; that he had converted this country from a field to a garden, this city from sticks to brick ; that the Navy was in an excellent way of restoring and reparation, that his Majesty laboured in nothing but want of money, and no offence so mortal as the misemployment of his treasure ; that concerning the business in hand he had little to say ", being in agreement with Lord Hubbard ; and so gave his vote for the mildest sentence proposed.

At night he attended state dinners. When Lady Hatton gave the great feast that was to reconcile her to the King and Buckingham, Bacon was one of the chief guests. Three days before he had been feasted with the judges by the College of Westminster and had distinguished himself by his munificence to the King's Scholars. There were countless entertainments at court, and he must have used York House for great occasions of display.

One interesting record of this period is four months of Bacon's private accounts, June to September, 1618. They are arranged under three heads—

receipts, gifts and rewards, payments. The receipts for the period are £4,160 12s. 10d. and consist to the extent of some £2,732 of fees from legal business. The other items only bear the names of the payers and it is uncertain for what services they were paid.

The gifts and rewards are very considerable. Some are tips: " To one that brought your Lordship cherries from Gorhambury—6/-." This is different from his mother's day when 6d. would have sufficed. " To Sir Robert Chichester's man that brought your Lordship a horse—£3, 6, 0." To another servant who brought twelve fat wethers—£2, 4, 0. To another who brought letters from London—5/-. Presents of all kinds flow into York House continuously—one sends a stag, another sweetmeats, his wife, who is staying at Gorhambury, sends her footman with fruit, and Sir Edward Carew offers boxes of orange flowers—and all the bearers of presents are tipped to a degree roughly proportionate to the value of the thing they brought and the dignity of the sender. Besides tips, Bacon gave much away as alms or gifts. Some of these gifts go to members of his own household—the groom of the footcloth receives £1, 2, 0. But more are alms. " To Goodman Fossey, a poor man—£1, 0, 0." "To a poor woman, one Knight's wife, by your Lp.'s order— £1, 2, 0." Schoolboys were remembered. " To Sergt. Finch his son and Mr. Johnson's son at Eton by your Lp.'s order—£1, 2, 0." And most famous entry of all—" To the washerwoman for sending after the crane that flew into the Thames—5/-." In all, during the four months, Bacon gave away £302, 7s.—not so very far from the traditional tithe— in alms.

The payments show large sums given to the steward for household expenses.

" July 9th   £400
  July 23rd   £200
  July 24th   £200
  July 26th   £100
  September 1st   £200 "

and so on—in all during the four months £1,800 was paid to the steward, while his Gorhambury household seemed to have cost about £400 during the same period. There are amusing items, which remind one that conditions of life were much the same then as now. On July 25th Bacon had one dozen handkerchiefs at 18s. and on September 23rd he needed two dozen more and two dozen socks at 9s. a dozen. In July he had a new suit. "Paid Christopher King his bill for making up your Lordship's last suit with all things belonging—£17, 19, 0." In August he paid £20 for a fair ruby set in a ring, and in August too he sat for his portrait and the artist received £33.

But the most remarkable thing was that Bacon was still in debt and paying interest on small sums at ten per cent. There are notices of interest paid on some four amounts totalling £700, so that he probably owed about £2,000 altogether. There are also notices of sums of money paid to tradesmen "on account", so that in spite of his vast prosperity he was by no means strictly solvent.

His expenses for the four months are £3,711 4s. 2d. and this added to his gifts makes his receipts exceed his expenditure for the period by a mere £150. There must certainly have been expenses which are not entered, e.g. the rent of York House, so tha

Bacon's indebtedness must have been slightly on the increase, even in these days of his glory.

These very heavy expenses are not surprising considering the size of his household. He had about a hundred servants in London and at least fifty— probably many more—at Gorhambury. They were for the most part magnificently dressed and their feeding alone must have been enormously expensive. Every now and then Bacon bethought him of his own precepts on economy and strove to make reductions. As a good start to the New Year in 1618, he " at one lap cashiered sixteen of his gallants ", and so notorious was his extravagance that the letter-writers of the day commented on this unusual economy.

If Bacon was in debt, his servants throve. Three are reported to have kept their own coaches, and several owned racehorses. His relations with his servant Hunt show both his determined carelessness in money matters and his habit of borrowing indiscriminately.

" He was wont to say to his servant Hunt (who was a notable thrifty man and loved this world, and the only servant he had that he could never get to become bound for him): The world was made for man, Hunt, and not man for the world. Hunt left an estate of £1,000 per annum in Somerset."

What Bacon really thought of all this life of greatness is clear from his Essays. He never freed himself from the dualism of actor and spectator, and whilst he pressed his claims for high office, transacted business with industry and acumen, prided himself on his skill and honour, he was yet capable of withdrawing from it all and of turning upon his whole

13

life the calm eye of dispassioned philosophy. The philosophy was the richer for his experience, and every sentence he wrote he wrote from his heart. But when he had written, seen the hollowness of his way of life and its vanity, he took it up again with the same skill and application.

The essay on *Great Place* was first written in 1607 when he was forty-seven and eagerly seeking the very greatness he saw to be so wearisome. He found his own words so true that when he revised it for the last time, after all his glory had fallen from him, he only thought it necessary to add a final paragraph. Bacon's understanding had been perfect from the beginning, his actions had been dictated by some other impulse.

" Men in Great Place are thrice servants, servants of the sovereign or state, servants of fame, and servants of business ; so as they have no freedom, neither in their persons, nor in their actions, nor in their times. It is a strange desire to seek power, and to lose liberty, and to seek power over others and to lose power over a main self. The rising into place is laborious, and by pains men come to greater pains ; and it is sometimes base, and by indignities men come to dignities ; the standing is slippery, and the regress is either a downfall or at least an eclipse, which is a melancholy thing.

" Nay, retire men cannot when they would, neither will they when it were reason, but are impatient of privateness, even in age and sickness which require the shadow . . .

" In place there is licence to do good and evil ; whereof the latter is a curse ; for in evil the best condition is not to will, the second not to can ; but power to do good is the true and lawful end of aspiring. For good thoughts (though God accept them) yet towards men they are little better than good dreams, except they be put in act, and that cannot be without power and place as the vantage and commanding ground."

Chapter XVIII

THE EXECUTION OF RALEIGH

In the next year of Bacon's Chancellorship there occurred one of the most pitiful episodes of English history : Raleigh's last voyage and execution. For thirteen years Raleigh had been a prisoner in the Tower, walking up and down on his little platform overlooking the river and the shipping, conducting simple chemical experiments, and writing a history of the world which ended at the triumph of L. Aemilius Paulus. The tides of time and politics went by him, and when at last he procured his release he was a political Rip van Winkle, who came forth on the age of James I with the ideas of Elizabeth.

Patriotic piracy was no more. As early as 1605 James had begun to suppress it.

" One Cockaine sent out a ship called the ' Merchant Royal ' this last summer, and got her to be entertained of the Duke of Florence to go against the Turks, in which service she took a great galleon of Constantinople of 1,200 ton called the ' Sultana ' and belonging to their queen mother, richly laden at Alexandria with inestimable wealth ; in which fight were slain 500 Turks and 300 more brought to Leghorn, the best of the goods taken out, the rest sunk with the galleon. For which piece of service our merchants stand in doubt to lose all their goods in Turkey, and to be debarred of their trade in those parts ; and Cockaine in the meantime lieth in the Fleet."

What occupation was it for a subject of King James, who for years had been trying to marry his daughter to a Spanish princess, to sail to America, attack a town, and meditate the old occupation of cruising upon the Plate fleet ?   Moreover, the great tradition was gone from the seas.   No commander had a perfect crew, but those that Raleigh managed to collect were worse than usual.   " What wonder is it (Raleigh wrote in his own excuse), being followed with a company of volunteers who for the most part had neither seen the sea nor the wars, who, some forty gentlemen excepted, had with me the very scum of the world, drunkards, blasphemers, and such others as their fathers, brothers, and friends thought it an exceeding good gain to be discharged of, with the hazard of some thirty, forty or fifty pounds, knowing they could not have lived a whole year so cheap at home : I say, what wonder is it that I have failed ? "

Raleigh was sixty-seven when he set out, weakened in body by age and imprisonment, deluded by imaginations, ignorant of the new way of the world.   He said that he was going to discover a gold mine in Guiana and he promised not to fight the Spaniards.   What he thought when he went, no one can know.   Perhaps, his mind on the past, he believed that success excuses all things, and, as he had once purchased Elizabeth's favour with the spoil of a Spanish carrick, so he hoped to buy James's with the gold of a mine.   Perhaps the restless longing of a prisoner had become more than he could bear, and like Essex he would " rather die than live in misery."

> Cowards fear to Die, but courage stout
> Rather than Live in Snuff, will be put out,

were his own " lines on a candle " before he died,

and after thirteen years, " no small space of mortal
life ", when hope of peaceful release there was none,
he may have deluded himself and attacked James on
his weakest point, his endless need of money.

What James and Buckingham thought when they
gave Raleigh permission to sail need hardly be
considered. In all probability they did not think at
all. If he succeeded or if he failed, they could
execute him, and Raleigh was not sufficiently important to occupy more than a fraction of their minds.
A bribe to Buckingham probably ensured James's
consent, and Buckingham was quite supremely
incapable of clear and intelligent thinking.

So Raleigh sailed, suffered all the tossings and
chances of an Atlantic voyage (and he was a man that
passionately hated the sea, though fate gave him fame
on it), failed to find his mine, and, while his men burnt
a Spanish village, lost his dearly-loved son. Thus
he came home broken in body and spirit, and disordered in judgment. When he might have fled
to France, he hesitated ; when his cousin Stukley was
ready to betray him, he attempted to flee ; and so
found himself once more in the Tower, facing the
stern row of examining lawyers who were trying to
prove that he had been involved in a plot with
France. James had got himself into trouble. The
Spanish ambassador, Gondomar, demanded reparation
for his master ; and James, who lacked the character
to resist, was quite willing to send Raleigh to be
hanged in Madrid. However, the Spanish Central
Government refused to accept such a melancholy
offering to international amity.

There was a legal difficulty about Raleigh's execution at home. He was still a prisoner under sentence,

and therefore in the opinion of Bacon and the other lawyers consulted he could not be tried for a new crime. Moreover, the King greatly feared his rhetoric and his power to influence popular feeling. It was decided, therefore, that Raleigh should be brought before a small committee, be accused of various crimes and told that, under the circumstances, the old sentence would be carried out. The speech of Montague, his judge, Coke's successor, was as dignified and kindly a piece of judicial rhetoric as could be found, and shows that if James cared nothing, Raleigh then as now was a touching figure to thinking men.

" I know that you have been valiant and wise ; I doubt not but you retain both these virtues, for now you shall have occasion to use them. I would give you counsel, but I know you can apply unto yourself far better than I can give you ; yet will I, with the good neighbour in the gospel, who, finding one on the way wounded and distressed, poured oil into his wounds and relieved him, give unto you the oil of comfort, though in respect that I am a minister of the law, mixed with vinegar. Sorrow will not avail you in some kind ; for, were you pained, sorrow would not ease you ; were you afflicted, sorrow would not avail you ; were you tormented, sorrow would not content you ; and yet the sorrow for your sins would be an everlasting comfort to you.

" Fear not death too much, nor fear not death too little ; not too much lest you fail in your hopes, not too little lest you die presumptiously.

" And here I must conclude with my prayers to God for it, and that he would have mercy on your soul."

Raleigh died on the scaffold with a return of his old gaiety. The graces of his age lasted him till his death, and his progress through the struggling crowd in Palace Yard till, " arms being spread ", he bid the executioner strike, was the conduct of a great actor. He mingled jests with earnest, a most elaborately prepared speech of justification with a natural carriage. His white hair and gallant bearing, his memories of the past and his contrast with the present, lifted him to the rank of martyr. James was never more disgraced than by that day's justice.

In an attempt to justify himself the King caused a full account of the matter to be written and published. It was an official apology such as had been produced after the death of Essex and it is probable that again it was mainly Bacon's work. It is a very fair specimen of a document of that kind, well-written, scrupulously fair, wherever we can check it, and moderate. It completely failed to influence public opinion. Raleigh had become and remained a martyr, and his own epitaph has prevailed over the most careful official prose.

> Even such is time, that takes in trust
> Our youth, our joys, our all we have,
> And pays us but with age and dust ;
>   Who in the dark and silent grave,
>   When we have wandered all our ways,
>   Shuts up the story of our days !
> But from this earth, this grave, this dust,
> The Lord shall raise me up, I trust !

CHAPTER XIX

THE *NOVUM ORGANUM*

BACON never allowed the essential dualism of his life to be interrupted for long. He might spend his days in legal business, his nights in official banquets, but he always found time to tend his health, enjoy the refined pleasures of sweet scents and quiet meditation, and to work at his philosophy. He had many rules for preventing the onset of age and the atrophy of his faculties. Some are merely medical, and were precautions which he had practised all his life, others show that he appreciated the part which an enjoyment of certain pleasures plays in health.

" In the third hour after the sun is risen, to take the air from some high and open place, with ventilation of *Rosae Moschatae* and fresh violets."

" Never to keep the body in the same posture above half an hour at a time."

" To break off custom. To shake off spirits ill disposed. To meditate on Youth. To do nothing against a man's genius."

Thus strengthened, amid all the bustle of London life, he published in 1620 the *Novum Organum*. What he hoped from it is told in the letter he sent to the King with his presentation copy.

" The work, in whatever colours soever it may be set forth, is no more but a new logic, teaching to invent and judge by induction (as finding syllogism incompetent for sciences of nature) and thereby to make philosophy and sciences both more true and more active.

"This tending to enlarge the bounds of Reason and to endow man's estate with new value, was no improper oblation to your Majesty, who, of men, is the greatest master of reason and author of benevolence.

"There be two of your council, and one other bishop of the land, that know I have been about some such work near thirty years, so as I make no haste. And the reason why I have published it now, specially being imperfect, is, to speak plainly, because I number my days and would have it saved. There is another reason for my so doing, which is to try whether I can get help in one intended part of my work, namely the compiling of a natural and experimental history, which must be the main foundation of a true and active philosophy . . .

"One thing I confess I am ambitious of, with hope, which is, that after these beginnings, and the wheel once set on going, men shall suck more truth out of Christian pens than hitherto they have done out of heathen."

In this last hope Bacon was premature. He was trying to set out the course which science was to follow, and as yet experimental science was unborn. When it did struggle into existence, its course was different from that which Bacon had imagined. The scheme which Bacon proposed was too formal. He imagines a vast organization where none existed, and his emphasis falls on the wrong points. In consequence, his elaborate system of induction, set out in axioms of extreme ingenuity and adorned with phrases that have remained to this day echoing down the corridors of thought, was barren of result.

We can understand the reason for this if we consider Bacon's exposition of the method. There were two defects in current thought that he hoped to remedy. In the first place, men would not look at nature but preferred, shut away from life and things, to spin from their own heads subtleties that were too fine to be useful. Spiders, Bacon called them. On the other hand, there were a few ants who amassed stores of raw facts and did not work at them. Bacon needed bees who would collect and transform. Secondly, because they ignored nature and man, and because their facts were so few, hypotheses were founded on the scantiest evidence, and the arguments and theories of the schools were often completely out of relation with observation.

Bacon wished to control nature for man's good, therefore man must understand nature, and to understand nature he must first observe her and collect his observations. Then he must form hypotheses as to the cause of the phenomena he observes, check these hypotheses against the observations, and so arrive at truth. This is roughly the practice of the sciences, but Bacon, being a lawyer, attempted to formalize the procedure so that, at a first glance, his account of it seems mechanical and artificial. Moreover, he says very little about hypothesis. This step seems to him so obvious that he misses its importance. He is more afraid that men will come to unfounded hypotheses than that they will not think of them at all, but if he is more inclined to restrain than encourage the making of hypotheses he clearly understands that they are necessary.

His example of induction is an investigation to discover the nature of heat. He begins by a table of things that are hot, starting with the sun and fire, and including animal heat, the burning of acids such as sulphuric, and the effects of alcohol on white of eggs. The second table consists of examples akin to the former which do not exhibit heat, e.g. the light of the moon and stars is not hot, though that of the sun is. The third table includes instances of things which vary in heat as the sun in winter and summer, or human beings when in normal health or in fevers, or the heat of flames from different burning substances. These three tables of presence, absence and variation are the raw material for induction. He then explains his method :[1]

" We are wont to term the office and use of these three tables the presenting a review of instances to the understanding, and when this has been done, induction itself is to be brought into action. For on an individual review of all the instances a nature is to be found, such as always to be present and absent with the given nature, to increase and decrease with it, and to form a more common limit of the nature. If the mind attempts this affirmatively from the first (which it always will when left to itself), there will spring up phantoms, mere theories and ill-defined notions, with axioms requiring daily correction. These will, doubtless, be better or worse, according to the power and strength of the understanding which creates them. But it is only for God, and perhaps for angels and intelligences, at once to recognize forms affirmatively at the first glance of contemplation : man, at least, is unable to do so, and is only allowed

[1] *Novum Organum* Bk. II, Aphorisms XV-XVII and XX.

to proceed first by negatives, and then to conclude with affirmatives, after every species of exclusion

" The first and almost perpetual precaution and warning which we consider necessary is this : that no one should suppose from the great part assigned by us to forms that we mean such forms as the meditations and thoughts of men have hitherto been accustomed to. . . . When we speak of forms, we mean nothing else than those laws and regulations of simple action which arrange and constitute any simple nature, such as heat, light, etc. The form of heat or form of light, therefore, means no more than the law of heat or the law of light. . . .

" We must now offer an example of the exclusion or rejection of natures found by the tables of review not to be of the form of heat. . . . For it is clear from what has been said that every contradictory instance destroys an hypothesis as to the form . . ."

Then follows a table showing what hypotheses as to the nature of heat can be rejected. That done :

" Since, however, truth emerges more readily from error than confusion, we consider it useful to leave the understanding at liberty to exert itself and attempt the interpretation of nature in the affirmative."

That is, the mind may now proceed to form an hypothesis which will fit the facts so gathered and sifted. Bacon, who had great powers of invention as well as thought, jumps at once to an answer which is approximately correct :

" From the instances taken collectively, as well as singly, the nature whose limit is heat appears to be motion. . . ." The particular motion which causes heat is :

(1) an expansive motion which

(2) tends towards the exterior, but at the same time bears the body upwards and

(3) is not a uniform expansive motion of the whole, but of the small particles of the body and

(4) is rapid.

When this hypothesis has been formed, the searcher after knowledge can test it by referring to his original observations, by making others and by devising experiments to test particular points.

That this account of scientific discovery is essentially true, any experimenter knows. Tables may not actually be drawn up as Bacon imagined, but the field is surveyed, previous work looked at, points thought of, rejected, revised, an hypothesis formed which fits the known facts, and then tested.

John Stuart Mill, writing more than two centuries later, when science was established, gives almost exactly the same account of the process. The only difference is that he has some completed experiments to offer as examples. It is marvellous that Bacon in the days before science existed should have foreseen so well what its method must be.

But if he foresaw the method, naturally he could not foresee the matter. Science has become too complicated, too specialized for his broad views. It has developed subtleties past his thought. Moreover, Bacon imagined that the chief work of science would lie in the collections of facts which would then be available for common use and scrutiny. He did not realize that the collections which he demanded would take a very different form. Each branch of science

has its own collections of facts available to the workers ; they are the data on which the science rests and
are the results of centuries of co-operative effort ;
they correspond to Bacon's tables of instances, but
they do not resemble them. Bacon was wrong
simply because he did not and could not know the
future.

Moreover, Bacon assumed too easily that hypotheses
would always be forthcoming. His own hypothesis,
given as an example, is a brilliant one ; but we know
today that it is hypotheses which are lacking more
often than facts. Bacon, from the character of his
own mind and the particular conditions of learning
in his own day, laid stress on what has proved the
less important part of the process.

Farther, for all Bacon's emphasis on experiment,
he was an indifferent experimenter. In this again he
stood merely as part of his age. The technique of
experiment had not been developed, and he was
trying sporadic experiments without any clear line
of investigation. Occasionally we have an experiment that he actually tried, and we can understand his
interest and delight as the phenomena are observed.

" Take a small wax candle, and put it in a socket of
brass or iron ; then set it upright in a porringer full
of spirit of wine heated ; then set both the candle and
the spirit of wine on fire, and you shall see the flame
of the candle open itself, and become four or five
times bigger than otherwise it would have been :
and appear in figure globular, and not in pyramis.
You shall see also that the inward flame of the candle
keepeth colour, and does not wax any whit blue
towards the outward flame of the spirit of wine.
This is a noble instance : wherein two things are

most remarkable : the one, that one flame within another quencheth not. . . . The other, that flame does not mingle with flame, as air does with air, but only remaineth contiguous."

Too often, however, Bacon thinks of the experiment but does not carry it out. His writings abound with the sentence, " It is a noble trial, and of very great consequence to try whether . . . " and then follows the description of an experiment he could easily have made, but which he had not attempted.

His most famous experiment, because of its tragic ending, concerned refrigeration ; and on the strength of the bronchitis, which followed a cold caught when the candle of his life was burning low, Bacon has been claimed, quite unjustifiably, as a martyr to experimental science.

" As he was taking the aire in a coach with Dr. Witherborne towards Highgate, snow lay on the ground, and it came into my Lord's thought, why flesh might not be preserved in snow, as in salt. They were resolved they would try the experiment presently. They allighted out of the coach and went into a poore woman's house at the bottom of Highgate Hill, and bought a hen and made this woman exenterate it, and then stuffed the body with snow, and my Lord did help to do it himself. The snow so chilled him that he immediately fell so extremely ill that he could not return to his lodgings (I suppose at Gray's Inn) but went to the Earl of Arundel's house at Highgate, where they put him into a good bed warmed with a pan, but it was a damp bed that had not been layn-in in about a yeare before, which gave him such a cold that in 2 or 3 days he dyed of suffocation."

It is part of Bacon's curious power that here as
elsewhere he should have seen so clearly what should
be done, and yet in himself have accomplished so
little ; and it is also part of the curious fortune of his
reputation, that his fame should be so closely linked
with experiment when he really did so little experimenting. But for the chance of his death after
exposure in the snow he would never have obtained
this posthumous glory.

Chapter XX

THE ACCUSATION

Bacon kept his sixtieth birthday at York House in high honour. To his feast came the court and nobility. Ben Jonson, as the leading poet of the day, recited verses in his honour, and he was raised a step in the peerage to become Viscount St. Albans.

These celebrations occurred amid anxious preparations at home and abroad. Frederick the Elector Palatine, the King's son-in-law, had become involved in the drunken and ambitious intrigues of the German princes. The revolted nobles of Bohemia had offered him the crown, and after many hesitations he had accepted it. No sooner had he done so and moved to Prague, than his own straggling dominions were threatened with invasion. On the north and west in particular, a Spanish army from the Netherlands was advancing, and it would only be by great exertions that it could be stopped. But meanwhile Ferdinand, who had the better claim to Bohemia, collected his allies and routed Frederick completely, so that the unhappy adventurer fled home from a dominion he had lost to one that he was about to lose.

The interest which his plight aroused in England had a double cause. He was a Protestant prince and his opponents were Catholics, and he was the King's son-in-law, husband of a popular princess and father of children who were looked upon with favour by the British nation. Moreover, the Spaniards were attacking the Palatinate, and, since Raleigh's death had proved that Englishmen might not fight the Spaniards by sea, any excuse was good enough to justify a war by land. If James had wanted to make himself popular, he had only to declare a Spanish war.

But this he would not do. He was still under the impression that he was going to marry his son to a Spanish princess, and he was completely dominated by the Spanish ambassador, Gondomar. Gondomar's influence was that of a brilliant, single-hearted statesman over an unstable, vain and foolish pedant. He had impressed his superior character and force so completely on James, that the King was unable to think for himself about any topic on which Gondomar meant to influence him. Thus the uneasy alliance with Spain continued, and James, through years of delays, insults and disappointments, continued to believe in the marriage he desired. In consequence, James refused to act vigorously about his son-in-law. He would certainly not support him in Bohemia. Kings were by God appointed, and James could not desert his class sufficiently to condone the usurpation of another man's throne. He did make an effort to discover, from a study of the ancient Bohemian Constitution, if Frederick's act was legal, but though he spent some months on the matter he could not discover precedents sufficiently clear to justify him in doing anything. But when Frederick was driven home again, he was inclined to be rather more active. He might almost have got to the point of a decisive action if Gondomar had not stood always at his elbow, threatening, cajoling, encouraging, and rendering the mind of a man never too fitted for public business hopelessly confused and unstable. The whole Spanish policy on the continent depended on the neutrality of

England, and Gondomar, with the assistance of that most useful fiction, the marriage treaty, succeeded very cleverly in maintaining it.

However, James did get as far as calling Parliament. His own finances, once they had been reduced to order, provided fairly well for his own needs, but a war, or even the threat of war, must be paid for out of the public purse. Bacon as usual wished Parliament to meet, and when it did meet took his part as Lord Chancellor in the pageantry.

Never had he been more easy nor more sure of himself. He had always been successful in parliament, and had for many years been the most respected member of the Lower House. There was no reason why his influence should have decreased. Though he now sat in the Woolsack he had done nothing to alienate any man's good opinion. Not only was he the same man, but he had received accessions of dignity and influence. He had every reason to be confident before both King and people.

Bacon's unchanging belief in the importance of Parliament, and his views on how it should be treated appear in the proclamation which he drew up for the King when the Parliament was proposed. The proclamation begins with a general survey of foreign affairs, stating that the King has always avoided wars, but that now he fears that he may be driven to engage in one. And in this event he will require help and counsel.

"For although the making of war or peace be a secret of empire, and a thing properly belonging to our high prerogative royal, and imperial power: yet never-the-less, in causes of that nature which we shall think fit not to reserve but to communicate, we shall ever think ourselves much assisted and strengthened by the faithful advice and general assent of our loving subjects."

If there is to be a war there must be money, and Bacon's next point is to ask the parliament to supply " some large and bountiful help of treasure." Further, as he believed that no parliament should meet for money alone, he sketches out other activities " upon these considerations, and for that also in respect of so long intermission of a parliament the times may have introduced something fit to be reformed, either by new laws or by the moderate desires of our loving subjects dutifully intimated unto us, we have resolved to hold a parliament."

The last section of the report contains suggestions as to the fittest men to be returned to parliament.

The proclamation did not please the King. Buckingham reports that the King, did not wish a proclamation " containing matter of state and the reasons for calling the parliament ; whereof the people are not capable." He therefore intended to use the last few paragraphs only. Bacon submitted to the mutilation of his proclamation and the change of his policy, merely remarking " I would not have thought of inserting matter of state for the vulgar, but that now-a-days there is no vulgar, but all statesmen."

Bacon clearly understood the trend of the times, which the King did not ; so that there was no reason why he should be disliked by a parliament which began its life in a more loyal frame of mind than any other of James' parliaments.

The next preparations which Bacon made for parliament were also prompted by an understanding of the Commons. He advised the King to revoke certain of the Patents which were the subjects of complaint. "We have chosen out," he wrote, "some that are most in speech, and do most tend either to the vexation of the common people, or the discontenting of the gentlemen and justices; the one being the original, the other the representative of the commons."

In a letter to Buckingham sent at the same time he mentions some of these patents by name "Your lordship may find that in the number of patents which we have represented to his majesty as likely to be stirred in by the Lower House of Parliament we have set down certain which may concern some of your Lordship's special friends. The one, that to Sir G. Monperson, touching the inns, the second to Mr. Christopher Villier and Mr. Maule, touching the recognisances for ale-houses.

These in duty could not be omitted, for that they are more rumoured, both by the vulgar and by the gentlemen, yea, and by the judges themselves, than any other patents at this day."

These patents concerning inns and ale-houses had already had a considerable history. It was felt then, as it is felt now, that inns and ale-houses should be licensed, and proper regulations made to ensure that they are run in a decent, orderly manner. The next question is who is to do the licensing. In the time of James I, as today, the Justices of the Peace had the duty and discharged it well or ill, according to their intelligence and diligence; and of their honesty there was little question. Now it had occurred to Monperson, an impecunious and ingenious relative of Buckingham's, that there was profit to be made out of the situation. The same thought occurs with great regularity to the police of Europe and America in dealing with various classes of the community today. He applied to the Court for a patent to make him the licensing authority for inns, pointed out that the Justices of the Peace now and then failed in their duties, and that under his administration all the defects of the present system would be removed. He could make out a fairly good case for his appointment, and the matter was naturally supported by the most powerful person in the state. The patent was apparently unexceptionable in law ; and as such Bacon and three other judges certified it. It was then passed on to a committee of five, who declared that it would be to the public good, and it was sealed by the King's special direction in the short interregnum between Ellesmere's death and Bacon's appointment to be Lord Keeper. We can quite well believe that all these certificates were true and honest. The trouble was that Monperson proceeded to use his power quite in the modern way, and evolved a system of blackmail on honest and dishonest innkeepers alike, making the first pay to avoid being accused of crimes they had not committed and the latter to avoid being accused of those they had. On this double traffic he throve, and the public indignation mounted. Now Bacon had never been asked if he thought the patent was for the public good, but only if he thought it legal, and this it apparently was. The referees to whom the more delicate question had been put might have answered that, considering the character of the man, they thought the power would be abused, but, as such an answer was in the circumstances unthinkable, they were compelled to look on the best side of the matter and hope that Monperson would do his duty.   Thus their certificate also was an honest one.

If these patents had been removed before parliament met much trouble would have been saved to all parties ; but Bacon's advice was again overruled, and James determined to let them stand till they were questioned, hoping apparently to rival Elizabeth's famous gesture over monopolies.   Unfortunately both men and times were changed.

In spite of all Bacon's preparations parliament met in a curious temper.   They were anxious to keep on good terms with the King and readily enough voted him two subsidies ; and though this was only £164,000 and no use for a war in the Palatinate, it was pleasant for the King to receive it, and implied good will. Less satisfactory was the conduct of the usual committee of grievances, which, appointed at the very opening of Parliament, had done what Bacon prophesied they would, and fallen at once upon the question of patents.

In the events which follow there is a strange determination about the behaviour of the House ; a studied selection in the objects and persons attacked ; a mingling of defference to the King with a violent assertion of privileges against his ministers.   All this suggests a personal policy very different from that likely to be possessed by the House as a whole.   The dominant person in the house of Commons was Sir Edward Coke, and the easiest way to understand what follows is to look on him as the instigator of his fellow-members.   Coke was not likely to forget that he was a privy councillor, and that his position depended on pleasing the King to some extent, nor was he likely to forget that in leading the House of Commons he possessed a power which at last made him superior to his old enemy, Bacon. The very first protests of the Commons against the patents passed beyond the facts, beyond the patentees, to the referees who had approved the original grants. Whilst Monperson and Mitchell, who were obviously guilty, were condemned; Bacon and the other referees, who were equally innocent of any fault, were attacked. But the attack would have been weak but for Sir Edward Coke.

At the first hint of the storm the policy of the King and Bacon was delay. By a timely adjournment of the House of Lords the conference between the two houses was postponed for a week. Bacon on the eve of this conference gives his views on the situation.

"I do hear from divers of judgment, that to-morrow's conference is like to pass in a calm, as to the referees. I woo nobody; I do but listen, and I have doubt only of Sir Edward Coke, who I wish had some round *caveat* given him from the King, as I think a word from the King mates him."

Bacon's information was correct; it was only Coke who made any attack on the referees, the other speakers greatly disappointing the hotheads of the party by coming "short in their task and not daring to touch matters to the quick concerning the referees."

In this and the ensuing conferences Bacon was in a position of the utmost delicacy. As Chancellor he must preside, ensure that the charges against himself received the most favourable hearing, report the results of the conference afterwards, and never say a word in his own defence. On the one occasion on which he did try to defend himself he was adjudged out of order, and had to apologize later, confessing " that contrary to the orders of the House, he had spoken at the last conference more than he had direction by the House to do : acknowledging that he had erred therein."

All Bacon's friends were now genuinely alarmed for his safety, but he himself still tried to believe in the armour of innocence.

" I would not have my friends too apprehensive either of me or for me ; for I thank God my ways are sound and good, and I hope God will bless me in them."

He certainly did not shrink from enquiry, and when at the next conference committees were appointed to study the matter further, Bacon himself proposed that the committees should begin by conferring with the three lawyers who had been most active in presenting the charges.

What the upshot of the matter would have been we do not know, for another and more convenient charge offering against Bacon, the whole matter of the referees was dropped ; and the house was off in full cry on another scent.

The first murmur of this trouble was a complaint about some junior officials in the Court of Chancery, but this was not a sufficient ground of action. Then a man named Awbry came forward saying that he had given Bacon a present for the better dispatch of suit, and close on the heels of this charge Edward Egerton appeared, and declared that the £400 which he had assured Bacon was a free present for the furnishing of his home, was really a bribe, and that he had not received value for his money. Bacon was in the extraordinary position of being accused by two discontented men because he had given them justice which had been upheld by every other court to which they had subsequently applied. They were angry that Bacon had taken the price of injustice and not performed his part of the bargain. As a fervent admirer once said of Kruger, " And look you, he is such an honest man that if you give him a bribe you are none the better for it," but Bacon's clients less discerning than the Dutchman, gave him no credit for his inconvenient honesty.

A scandal against the Lord Chancellor suited everybody. It would ruin the chief supporter of the King's prerogative without directly attacking the King, it would ruin Bacon personally, it might diminish the power of the Court of Chancery which was still obnoxious to its legal rivals. The House of Commons at once formed a committee to investigate the matter, and information was invited. Bacon was horrified, but, secure in his own innocence. He wrote to Buckingham : " Your lordship spake of purgatory. I am now in it, but my mind is in a calm ; for my fortune is not my felicity. I know I have clean hands and a clean heart ; and I hope a clean house for friends or servants. But Job himself, or whosoever was the justest judge, by such hunting of matters against him as hath been used against me, may for a time seem foul, specially in a time when greatness is the mark and accusation is the game. And if this be to be a Chancellor, I think if the great seal lay upon Hounslow Heath, nobody would take it up."

All this had come very suddenly, so suddenly that in the greatest crisis of his life Bacon was almost dumb. On the 12th March the Commons were still occupied with the question of the referees. Bacon on the Woolsack, embarrassed but secure. On the 19th, after only a week's interval, the Lords were debating the charge of corruption preferred by the Commons, and Bacon was ill, prostrated in body by the break up of his whole scheme of life. It is a shock for the man who knows himself guilty to find justice on his track, but it is a far greater shock for a man who held himself spotless, the " justest Chancellor since his father's day," to find himself accused of the very crimes which he would most abominate and despise. Bacon suffered more cruelly from the blow to his self-esteem and from the shattering of his own ideal self, than he could have done from any other cause.

His letter to the King is full of his bewilderment.

" When I enter into myself, I find not the materials of such a tempest as is comen upon me. I have been (as your majesty knoweth best) never author of any immoderate counsel. I have been no avaricious oppressor of the people. I have been no haughty or intolerable or hateful man, in my conversation or carriage. I have inherited no hatred from my father, but am a good patriot born. Whence should this be ? For these are the things that are to raise dislikes abroad.

For the House of Commons, I began my credit there, and now it must be the place of sepulture thereof ; and yet this parliament, upon the message touching Religion, the old love revived, and they said I was the same man still, only honesty was turned into honour.

For the Upper House, even within these days before these troubles, they seemed to take me into their arms, finding in me ingenuity which they took to be the true straight line of nobleness, without crooks or angles.

And for the briberies and gifts wherewith I am charged, when the books of hearts shall be opened, I hope I shall not be found to have the troubled fountain of a corrupt heart in a depraved habit of taking rewards to pervert justice; howsoever I may be frail, and partake of the abuses of the times."

This is the case as it appeared in all sincerity to Bacon, and to his shame, mental agony, and anxiety was added deep bewilderment and a genuine failure to understand how it had all happened. Unless we regard Coke as the moving spirit that bewilderment must still remain.

Bacon was too ill to take his place in parliament and wrote to the Lords apologizing for his absence. " It is no feigning nor fainting, but sickness both of my heart and of my back, though joined with that comfort of mind, that persuadeth me that I am not far from heaven, whereof I feel the first fruits. And because whether I live or die, I should be glad to preserve my honour and fame, as far as I am worthy; hearing that some complaints of bribery are come before your Lordships, my request unto your Lordships are :

" First that you will maintain me in your good opinion, without prejudice, until my cause be heard; secondly that . . . your Lordships would give me some convenient time to advise with my counsel; thirdly that I may be allowed to except to the witnesses brought against me, and to move questions to your Lordships for their cross-examination, and likewise to produce my own witnesses for the discovery of the truth; and lastly, if there come any more petitions of the like nature, that your Lordships would be pleased not to take any prejudice or apprehension of any number or muster of them, especially against a judge that makes two thousand decrees and orders in a year, but that I may answer them, according to the rules of justice, severally and respectively."

None of these most reasonable petitions was granted ; and the Lords in Bacon's absence continued to collect evidence, so framing the interrogatives on which the witnesses were examined as to encourage all information by a grant of impunity to the witness, and to collect the maximum amount of evidence against the Chancellor by treating the giving of a present as the same as the giving of a bribe. What would have happened to this evidence under cross-examination we do not know. It was never put to the test, but as much of it came from an arch-rascal, whom Bacon himself had removed from his place, it was probably very flimsy.

In the month's cessation of business which Easter brought, Bacon went down to Gorhambury. He was ill, and he believed, at times hoped, that he was dying. He still did not know details of the charges brought against him, so could do nothing to prepare his defence, and thus despairing of earth he turned his mind to heaven. He drew up the two documents which a man of his period and in his situation might naturally write, a will and a prayer. The will is simple, the opening clauses impressively so.

" I bequeath my soul to God above, by the oblation of my Saviour.

My body to be buried obscurely.

My name to the next ages and to foreign nations."

His papers and books go to his brother, his jewels and trinkets to his wife or friends.

" All my lands, tenements and hereditaments, leases,

goods and chattels . . . I give and bequeath to my executors for the payment of my debts by their discretion, and the surplusage of the value of them to be disposed as follows."

Then follow legacies of £500 and £800 to secretary and servants and the " rest *in pios usus* to be distributed at the discretion of my executors."

This very modest will, which indicates a man shuffling off the cares of life and not straining himself to control the future, even as regards his own fame, is accompanied by a prayer which contains very much the same attitude. . . . " Remember (O Lord) how thy servant hath walked before thee : remember what I have first sought, and what hath been the principal in mine intention. I have loved thy assemblies, I have mourned for the divisions of thy Church; I have delighted in the brightness of thy sanctuary. . . . The state and bread of the poor and oppressed have been precious in mine eyes ; I have hated all cruelty and hardness of heart. I have (though in a despised weed) procured the good of all men. . . . Thy creatures have been my books, but thy Scriptures much more. I have sought thee in the courts, fields and gardens, but I have found thee in thy temples. . . .

" And now when I thought most of peace and honour, thy hand is heavy upon me, and hath humbled me, according to thy former loving kindness, keeping me still in thy fatherly school, not as a bastard but as a child.

" Besides my innumerable sins, I confess before thee that I am debtor to thee for the gracious talent of thy gifts and graces, which I have neither put into a napkin, nor put it (as I ought) to exchangers, where it might have made best profit ; but misspent it in things for which I was least fit, so as I may truly say, my soul hath been a stranger in the course of my pilgrimage.

" Be merciful unto me, O Lord, for my Saviour's sake, and receive me into thy bosom or guide me in thy ways."

This prayer, so characteristic of Bacon, with his love of brightness and gardens, and his hankering after the scholar's life which he had put by, is the true surrender of his life of power and place.

Chapter XXI

THE SUBMISSION

WHEN the House met again, Bacon realized that his case with the Lords was hopeless. Though all the world was talking of his crimes, though evidence was being collected and discussed, he had not yet received any definite statement of the charges brought against him, nor had he or his representative been allowed to attend at any meeting or to cross-examine the witnesses. The little committees of four who had charge of the different items of the charge were honest men but quite unlearned in the law, and their presentation of the evidence was, in effect, the final judgment; and this was given after hearing only the evidence for the prosecution, and at a time too of fierce political feeling.

Bacon therefore never had any chance to make a formal defence, but that he could have made it on various grounds we can see from scattered passages. He never intended, however, to make it in a factious spirit. From the moment when the charge was first mooted his language had been the same.

" I am resolved, when I come to my answer, not to trick up my innocency by cavillations or voidances, but to speak to them the language that my heart speaketh to me, in excusing, extenuating or ingenuous confessing; praying to God to give me the grace to see to the bottom of my faults, and that no hardness of heart do steal upon me."

His real defence was the nature and intention of his acts and the customs of the times. When the Lords began to collect evidence, their interrogatories ran :

1. Whether they, by themselves or any other person, have given money or other gratuity to the Lord Chancellor, or to any other servants, friends or followers of his ?

2. Whether they have advised or directed any so to do, or known of any other that hath so done ?

3. Whether they, or the parties which they advised so to do, or have heard so to have done, had then any cause or suit depending before him, or intended to have any ?

4. Whether they have intended, attempted, or contracted for any gratuity so to be given, though not performed ?

Bacon would have begun at once by distinguishing the cases.

" These be three degrees or cases of gifts and rewards given to a judge.

" The first is, of bargain, contract, or promise of reward, *pendente lite*. And this is properly called *venalis sententia*. And of this my heart tells me I am innocent, that I had no bribe or reward in my eye or thought, when I pronounced any sentence or order.

" The second is, a neglect in the judge to inform himself whether the cause be fully at an end or no, what time he receives the gift, but takes it upon the credit of the party that all is done, or otherwise omits to enquire.

" And the third is, when it is received *sine fraude*, after the cause ended, which, it seems by the opinion of the civilians, is no offence."

So much for the general principle. For his own particular case, if he had erred in taking gifts of the second class, he could plead that during his four-year tenure of the office some 8,000 orders and decrees had been made by him, and that no man could be expected to remember clearly at what stage each one was, and further these were the customs of the day. " I must likewise confess to your Majesty that at new year's tides, and likewise at my first coming in (which was as it were my wedding), I did not so precisely as perhaps I ought examine whether those that presented me had causes before me, yea or no."

When all this is taken into consideration, the manner of collecting the charge, the lack of criticism of the witnesses, the circumstances of the time, it is amazing that Bacon only finds it necessary to admit four cases in which he definitely took a present *pendente lite*, and never with the smallest corrupt purpose or intent. It is equally surprising that, all told, the Lords could only rake up 28 charges of any sort or kind, though they gave every encouragement to evidence at second-hand, and though the conditions of examination were highly favourable to perjury.

Bacon, when he saw his case was hopeless with the Lords, appealed for an audience with the King, which was granted, but profited him nothing ; the King refusing to commit himself in any way. The next question was how best to meet the blow. Bacon realized he must lose the Seal that had come to him as a bride (served for and longed for as a Rachel), but he hoped that he could avoid any further punishment. For his own comfort he collected precedents of other high transgressors and compared their crimes with his own, hoping that, as his was a slight error, so his punishment might also be slight. He reflected also on such cases as those of Somerset and his lady, and decided that, as he could not hope to secure an acquittal in the present state of public feeling, he had most hope by making a general confession and craving mercy.

He therefore wrote to the Lords in general terms, saying that he had not yet received a formal note of the charges brought against him, but, having understood their nature from general talk, he found " matter sufficient and full, both to move me to desert the defence, and to move your Lordships to condemn and censure me."

He begged that in mercy his punishment might be confined to the loss of the Seal, and hinted that he was being made a martyr to the public good, the great example on which the future purity of the courts should be founded.

This letter was not at all to the Lords' taste. It was not sufficiently humble, it suggested that their Lordships were being precipitate or harsh, and it indicated that Bacon could have made quite a good defence if he would. They wanted something very different, and wrote and told Bacon so. " That the Lord Chancellor's confession is not fully set down by his Lordship in the said submission for three causes : (1) his Lordship confesseth not any particular bribe nor corruption ; (2) nor showeth how his Lordship heard of the charge thereof ; (3) the confession, such as it is, is afterwards extenuated in the same submission, and therefore the Lords have sent him a particular of the charge, and do expect his answer to the same, with all convenient expedition."

It was only after this that Bacon saw the charges against him, and they were sent him in an abbreviated form which gave him little opportunity to examine their truth. Still he was prepared to confess anything in reason, and returned the paper confessing the articles, all but two, and stating that with four exceptions the money had been taken as a present at the end of the suit.

The nature of the charges and confessions can be seen from two examples, one where the present was received at the end of the suit—after the general fashion of the day, and one where the present was *pendente lite* and therefore in Bacon's own opinion culpable.

" To the third article of the charge, videlicet, in the case between Hodie and Hodye, he received a douzen of buttons of the value of fifty pounds about a fortnight after the case ended.

" I confess and declare, that as it is laid in the charge, about a fortnight after the cause was ended (it being a suit of great inheritance) there were gold buttons about the value of fifty pounds as is mentioned in the charge, presented unto me, as I remember by Sir Thomas Perient and the party himself.

" To the fourth article of the charge, videlicet, in the case between the Lady Wharton and the heirs of Sir Francis Willoughby, he received of the Lady Wharton three hundred and ten pounds.

" I confess and declare, that I received of the Lady Wharton, at two several times (as I remember) in gold, two hundred pounds and a hundred pieces ; and this was certainly *pendente lite* : but yet I have a vehement suspicion that there was some shuffling between Mr. Shute and the Register in entering some orders, which afterwards I did distaste."

In plain fact Lady Wharton and her assistants had done everything in their power to interfere with the course of justice and failed.

This confession was enough for the Lords ; they

decided that Bacon was guilty, in a general way, of corruption. The next stage was his punishment. Here precedents failed them, but after some desultory bickering round the House it was decided with one dissentient voice, Buckingham's, that he should pay a fine of £40,000, be imprisoned during the King's pleasure in the Tower, be incapable of any office, place or employment in the State or Commonwealth, and never be allowed to sit in Parliament, or to come within the verge of the court. He was left his honours ; the Seal had, of course, already gone.

This happened on May 3rd. Thus in the space of some six weeks Bacon ceased to be the most important official of the realm, and became a man unable to pay his creditors, without fortune or hope, and banished from all that he cared for. The verge of the court was a circle of radius twelve miles, and so long as the court was in London Bacon was cut off from all society, all learned intercourse, as complete an exile from his life and interests as Cicero at the court of Thessalonica.

Buckingham having voted in Bacon's favour, the King did what he could to mitigate the sentence. Bacon spent two days in the Tower, that being the duration of his Majesty's pleasure, and then went to stay with a friend at Fulham and recover his health. His monetary problems were also eased by the King. If in the height of his prosperity Bacon was always borrowing and in debt, this sudden and complete collapse of his fortune left him not only with his past debts unpaid, but with new commitments which he had no means of meeting. From his creditors the King could and did protect him by a legal fiction. The fine due to the crown took priority over all other

claims, and till that was paid, which by arrangement
it was not, no one else could take action.

In June Bacon was compelled to go to Gorhambury
and there, cut off from friends, from the best libraries,
and from all chance of helping himself in his troubles,
he remained for several months, writing letters to his
friends and trying to devise some means for his material
existence. His financial difficulties were endless and
acute. Nothing stood between him and absolute
ruin but the fine which the King did not exact; and
for his day to day expenses he was dependent on a
very small pension irregularly paid. At one time for
his sustenance he applied for the Provostship of Eton,
but it was not granted; and this miserable financial
worry was inexpressibly wretched to a man of Bacon's
tastes and magnificent past.

Worse, because it hurt him more, was the prohibi-
tion to come to London, and Bacon sued in vain for
its removal. Buckingham wrote and told him that
the King refused, but as the very next sentence of the
letter concerns Bacon's refusal to give up the lease of
York House, no one could doubt the reason why the
King had not thought fit to grant the request. Indeed
Buckingham had set his mind on having York House,
and when he had so decided no consideration of God
or man was likely to dissuade him from it. Bacon
clung to the house, his birthplace, the setting of his
greatness, the reminder of what he once had been, and
he would not at first let it go. But Buckingham had
a strong weapon. Bacon out of London languished.
If he was allowed to return for a few weeks, there was
always the threat of a new expulsion—there was
always the tantalizing longing for the old way of life,
and then the return to the country and solitude.

" Here I live," he wrote in a cold December, " upon the sword-point of a sharp air, endangered if I go abroad, dulled if I stay within, solitary and comfortless without company, banished from all opportunities to treat with any to do myself good, and to help out my wrecks ; and that which is one of my greatest griefs, my wife, that hath been no partaker of my offending, must be partaker of this misery of my restraint."

It was now that he tasted the full sweets of dis-interested friendship, as well as the bitterness of successful hostility. Toby Matthew, his life-long friend, was his agent in London, his servant Meautys journeyed backwards and forwards, a faithful inter-mediary, even Gondomar, the Spanish ambassador, showed the respect in which he had held the Lord Chancellor by setting out his case to the King. But Buckingham was stronger than all these. York House he would have, and till he had it Bacon should never be released from his restraint. The position was made all the more difficult for Bacon because the new Lord Chancellor, Bishop Williams, was his enemy and put every obstacle in the way of granting the con-cessions Bacon asked. It was perhaps of him that Bacon thought when he added to his essay on *Great Place* the last sentences. " Use the memory of thy predecessor fairly and tenderly. For if thou do not, it is a debt will sure be repaid when thou art gone."

But at last the delicate negotiation was concluded, Bacon signed away the lease of his house to Bucking-ham's nominee, and received in return permission to return to London.

Bacon's King had deserted him ; his God was more constant.

CHAPTER XXII

THE CONSOLATION OF PHILOSOPHY

THERE are few things in life more impressive than an ageing philosopher. With his time growing short, with neither fame nor wealth to prove to him that his work has been good, he presses on with an unflagging energy that uses as a spur the thought of approaching death. There is so little time and so much to be done. The great work that is to stand *aere perennius* is so incomplete. If the stones lie handy, they require so much shaping, and the edifice that is to prove the triumph of mind over nature or the universe is for ever developing fresh towers, new battlements, and the worker, the Shadow ever behind him, meticulously fits stone to stone, polishes the smooth lintels and evens the fair flagstones.

Bacon had never, all through his life, been unheedful of his great projects. Slowly, year by year, he had accumulated his materials, planned and replanned the work. He lived his life so as to extract from himself the maximum results. His memory was extraordinary and did not fail him. He was no thoughtless man who shuts himself away with books and reads till he is dazzled in mind and wasted in body; he took his exercise, walked, rode gently, played at bowls, and then, without losing time, took out his books and began.

His mind was so well organized that he could carry a thread of philosophic thought subconsciously through the business of the day and, so soon as he was free, return to it and elaborate it. At night, as in the days of his youth, he lay and meditated *nescio quid* (unless he took a draught of strong beer to make him sleep), but with the years he became, as other middle-aged men are, an early riser, and in the morning dictated what he had thought on in the night.

His writing was both his hobby and a duty he owed to himself, to mankind and to God. Even when health failed him for serious composition he was not idle, but took in hand the translation of some one of his books into Latin, or even, when he was too ill even for such routine work, dictated collections of apothegms or translations of the Psalms.

When the break-up of his political life first threatened, his immediate thought was literature. Before the Lords had begun to consider their sentence, he wrote to the King.

" But because he that hath taken bribes is apt to give bribes, I will go farther and present your Majesty with a bribe. For if your Majesty give me peace and leisure, and God give me life, I will present your Majesty with a good history of England and a better digest of your laws."

Thus Bacon's first work after his sentence was a history of Henry VII, one of the best pieces of historical writing in English. It was written by a man disordered in health, broken in fortune, harassed by every kind of financial difficulty. To write it was both Bacon's consolation and the triumph of his mind over his fortunes. Bacon was released from the Tower by June 4th, 1621. The history was finished and sent to the King on October 8th, the work occupying only four months, which must have been the most shattering in his whole existence. Thucydides wrote his history in exile ; Bacon produced his before the ink was dry on his sentence of banishment.

For this work he had access to the great library collected by Sir Robert Cotton, which is now in the British Museum. One of the greatest tribulations of being banished to Gorhambury was that, by depriving him of access to this library, it made it impossible for him to continue his historical work. How bitter such a state of things is every scholar knows.

Bacon when he wrote of Henry VII, was peculiarly fitted for the task. There was a sympathy between the men. Bacon brought to the work a deep knowledge of law, a profound experience of men and affairs. He wrote as one statesman of another, and his judgments have never been questioned. His style can at times achieve perfection and his closing paragraph is one of the most beautiful ever written in English.

" He was born at Pembroke Castle, and lieth buried at Westminster, in one of the stateliest and daintiest monuments of Europe, both for the Chapel, and for the sepulchre. So there he dwelleth more richly dead, in the monument of his tomb, than he did alive in Richmond, or any of his palaces. I could wish he did the like in this monument of his fame."

More insistent, even than history, were the claims of philosophy, because philosophy was his life's love, and residence at Gorhambury was not so fatal to that as the other. Bacon, with his singular persistence, returned once more to his vast scheme.

Writing to a foreign correspondent a year before his death, he sets out his plans and his faith. " The first volume consists of books concerning the *Advancement of Learning*, and this, as you know, is already published and includes the partitions of the sciences, which is the first part of my *Instauration*. After this will follow the *Novum Organum*, to which there is yet a second part to be added—but I have already compassed and planned it out in my mind. And in this manner the second part of the *Instauration* will be completed. As for the third part, namely, the *Natural History*, that is plainly a work for a King or Pope, or some college or order, and cannot be done as it should be by a private man's industry. And those portions which I have published, concerning *Winds* and concerning *Life and Death*, are not history pure, because of the axioms and greater observations that are interposed, but a kind of writing mixed of natural history and a rude and imperfect intellectual machinery, which is the fourth part of the *Instauration*. Next therefore will come the fourth part itself, wherein will be shown many examples of this machine, more exact and more applied to the rules of induction. In the fifth place will follow the book that I have entitled the *Precursors of the Second Philosophy*, which will contain my discoveries concerning new axioms, suggested by the experiments themselves, that they may be raised as it were and set up, like pillars that were on the ground. And this I have set down as the fifth part of my *Instauration*. Last comes the *Second Philosophy* itself—the sixth part of the *Instauration*, of which I have given up all hope, but it may be that the ages and posterity will make it flourish.

" I have, you see, high hopes with small means.

" Conamur tenues grandia.

" But my hope is this—that these things appear to

proceed from the providence and infinite goodness of God. First because of the ardour and constancy of my own mind, which in this pursuit has not grown old nor cooled in so great a space of time, it being now forty years, as I remember, since I composed a juvenile work on this subject, which with great confidence and a magnificent title I named ' The Greatest Birth of Time '. Secondly because it seems, by reason of its infinite utility, to enjoy the sanction and favour of God, the all-good and all-mighty."

These are magnificent words from a man of sixty-four whom the world might hold broken by his misfortunes. The true philosopher, whatever he may do at times, has always an impregnable fortress to which he can retire. It is a legend, truer than most, that when faced with death he reads the *Phædo*, and when his world falls about him he stands, like the virtuous man, unmoved among the ruins. Bacon, when he passed to his philosophy, was a different being from the ready, astute civil servant, a different man from the lover of glass balls, purple velvet, or the wavering lights reflected from rippling water. His eyes had the shine of the believer, his voice the ring of the prophet, his mind the neat precision of the expert craftsman. The last few years of his life have for their true history the race with death, and his monument is the mass of writings he left behind him.

In 1622, when the *Novum Organum* was but half written, Bacon turned to making collections of natural history to provide the material on which his further arguments might be built, and he vowed that every month should see one completed. It was a proud attempt, worthy of one who had taken

" all knowledge for his province " while still in the twenties, and for one month he carried out his intention. The history of *Winds* appeared. Then he took up the subject of *Life and Death*, with the hope of inspiring physicians to treat their craft in a more scientific way. This proved more lengthy, and full three months passed before the book was ready ; and then Bacon's mind swung back to its old paths of politics for a moment, and he produced a paper on the best means to control the rate of interest, and the monthly succession was stayed, and the great work remained in his hands.

What Bacon hoped from science and philosophy is clear. To his mind they were twin sisters, not yet divided into the Martha and Mary of the intellectual world ; but all his scattered sayings are collected and given the force of a vision in his *New Atlantis*, the fable of the perfect state where the scientist is ruler. Bacon never wrote more beautiful and vivid prose, never put together a more perfect expression of life as he dreamed it might be lived than in this fragment. In this land of wisdom there is peace and goodwill, knowledge harnessed to man's need, and the vices of his day destroyed. There are no bribes nor presents, and the rule is to the wise, and the state lies in the hands of righteousness. It is a less military Utopia than Plato's, more comfortable, more kindly. It is far more intellectual than More's, and it has what is so rare among ideal commonwealths, the shine of colours and velvets, the charm of pomp, and the graciousness of luxury.

No one can read the *New Atlantis* without appreciating the dream of its author. His other writings, and those on which he most prided himself, fall dead today.

James declared that the *Novum Organum* was " like the peace of God—it passeth understanding ", and that solid tome, for all the care of an editor, has ceased to be a set book for Oxford Greats. But reading in the later books of the *Advancement of Learning*, one sees Bacon as the true founder of the two departments of philosophy on which England most prides herself, psychology and ethics. Bacon, first of the modern world, looked full at facts. His temper of mind, when he deals with man and thoughts, is that of Hobbs and Locke. One catches notes that belong to *Leviathan* or the *Essay on Human Understanding*. Bacon had foreseen the complete study of man, body and mind, which is modern psychology ;[1] he had seen the defects of intellectualist ethics.[2]   As he walked and talked with Hobbs, the clever young man listening to the old one, the true movement of English thought for the next century was born amid the gardens of Gorhambury.

At the end of his life, Bacon was back in his old chambers of Gray's Inn.   The circle of Fortune was rounded, and as he looked out on the gardens he had planned and planted, he wrote the last of his essays in the same room in which he had written the first. In these later essays his style is less epigrammatic ; he allows his fancy to wander, imagining in detail the perfect house and garden.   But most famous are his final thoughts on friendship.   They are coldly phrased, but they are the expression of a love that had lasted through life and endured the deepest changes of fortune on both sides.   Toby Matthew had been imprisoned and exiled for a change of religion ;

[1] *De Augmentis Scientiarum*, Bk. IV, 1, 3.
[2] *De Augmentis Scientiarum*, Bk. VII, 1, 2, 3.

Bacon had been disgraced and ruined, yet neither, in good fortune or bad, ever deserted the other. Bacon, cautious, exact, writes : " A principal fruit of friendship is the ease and discharge of the fullness of the heart, which passions of all kinds do cause and induce. . . . No receipt openeth the heart but a true friend, to whom you may impart griefs, joys, fears, hopes, suspicions, counsels and whatsoever lieth upon the heart to oppress it, in a kind of civil shrift or confession. . . .

" The second fruit of friendship is healthful and sovereign for the understanding, as the first is for the affections ; for friendship maketh indeed a fair day in the affections from storm and tempest, but it maketh daylight in the understanding, out of darkness and confusion of thoughts. . . .

" After these two noble fruits of friendship followeth the last fruit, which is, like the pomegranate, full of many kernels ; I mean aid and bearing a part in all actions and occasions. . . . Men have their time, and die many times in desire of some things which they principally take to heart. If a man have a true friend, he may rest secure that the care of those things will continue after him, so that a man hath, as it were, two lives in his desires. A man hath a body, and that body is confined to a place ; but where friendship is, all offices of life are, as it were, granted to him and his deputy. A man cannot speak to his son but as a father, to his wife but as a husband, to his enemy but upon terms ; whereas a friend may speak as the case requires, and not as it sorteth with the person."

A man who wrote that had found a noble and faithful friend, and knew it. That he was also himself noble and faithful is clear from Toby Matthew's description of him :

"And I can truly say (having had the honour to know him for many years as well when he was in his lesser fortunes as now that he stands at the top in the full flower of his greatness) that I never yet saw traces in him of a vindictive mind, whatever injury were done him, nor ever heard him utter a word to any man's disadvantage which seemed to proceed from personal feeling against the man, but only (and that too very seldom) from judgments made of him in cold blood.   It is not his greatness that I admire, but his virtue ; it is not the favours I have received from him (infinite though they be) that have thus enthralled and enchained my heart, but his whole life and character, which are such that, if he were of inferior condition, I could not honour him the less, and if he were my enemy I should not the less love and endeavour to serve him."

Bacon died of bronchitis in 1626 when he was sixty-five.   He was buried, as he wished, obscurely, and his name, left to the next ages and foreign nations, has been treated strangely.   Some hold him for the greatest Lord Chancellor of England and a noble philosopher ; others revile him as a man who failed to live up to the hypocritical standards of the Victorian age ; and yet others, working on him as the Middle Ages worked on Virgil, have transformed him into a sorcerer who alternately wrote masterpieces of poetic drama and invented acrostics for unoccupied pedants to decipher.   When we see Bacon in the motley of his reputation—Chancellor's gown, the scholar's bands, as the raving poet and the magician-priest of the Rosicrucians, we are amazed at the disappearance of the honest, faithful friend and devoted civil servant. Happier perhaps is his loved Gorhambury, which has been left alone, where the sheep now crop the rough grass where his exquisite gardens lay, and a scanty rail protects the last ruins of his mansion from the prying of an infrequent tourist.

BIBLIOGRAPHY

ARENSBERG, W. C. *The Secret Grave of Francis Bacon at Lichfield.* 1923. San Francisco.

—— *Burial of Francis Bacon and his Mother in the Lichfield Chapter House.* 1924. Pittsburg.

BIRCH, DR. THOMAS. *Memoirs of Queen Elizabeth.* 1754. London.

Court and Times of James I. 1848. London.

D'EWES, SIR SIMONDS. *Journals.* 1682. London.

DOUTHWAITE, W. R. *Gray's Inn.* 1886. London.

GOODMAN, BISHOP G. *Court of King James I.* 1839.

GARDINER, S. R. *History of England, 1603-1642.* 1883-4. London.

—— *Prince Charles and the Spanish Marriage.* 1869. London.

—— *What Gunpowder Plot was.* 1897. London.

GIBBS, SIR PHILIP. *Romance of George Villiers.* 1930. London.

HOLDSWORTH, W. S. *History of English Law.* 1922. London.

HOWELL, T. B. *State Trials,* Vol. I. 1809. Vol. II. 1816. London.

JARDINE, DAVID. *Reading on the Use of Torture in England.* 1837. London.

—— *Criminal Trials.* 1832. London.

LATHAM, AGNES MARY. *The Poems of Sir Walter Raleigh.* 1929. London.

LODGE, EDMUND. *Portraits of Illustrious Personages.* 1823. London.

MONTAGU, BASIL. *Works of Bacon.* 1825-36. London.

MACAULAY, LORD. *Essays.* 1850. London.

OLDYS, W. *Life of Raleigh.* 1736. London.

RIMBAULT, E. F. *Works of T. Overbury.* 1856. London.

STRACHEY, GILES LYTTON. *Elizabeth and Essex.* 1928. London.

SPEDDING, JAMES. *Letters and Life of Lord Bacon.* 1862. London.

ELLIS and SPEDDING. *Works of Lord Bacon.* 1857-62. London.

STRYPE, JOHN. *Annals of the Reformation.* 1709. London.

THEOBALD, BERTRAM G. *Francis Bacon, Concealed and Revealed.* 1930. London.

WALDMAN, MILTON. *Sir Walter Raleigh.* 1927. London.

YOUNGHUSBAND, SIR GEORGE. *The Tower of London.* 1924. London.

INDEX

DATE DUE